DI DI MAU

A TRUE STORY ABOUT

TIGERS, ROCK APES, THE JUNGLE, AND WAR

DARREN WALTON

with Michael J. Coffino

**Di Di Mau: A True Story About Tigers,
Rock Apes, the Jungle, and War**
Darren Walton with Michael J. Coffino
©2023, Darren Walton. All rights reserved.
Published by BATT Publishing, San Rafael, California

ISBN 979-8-9886359-2-5 (hardcover)
ISBN 979-8-9886359-0-1 (paperback)
ISBN 979-8-9886359-1-8 (eBook)
Library of Congress Control Number: 2023917247

Publication managed by AuthorImprints.com

This book is dedicated to the late Corporal J. L. Wiley, a special friend and phenomenal team leader. I was honored you selected me as point man for our recon unit, and I was honored and blessed to be your buddy. I know Jerry and Gregg miss you terribly, just as much as I do. Semper Fi.

TABLE OF CONTENTS

DISCLOSURE

This book reflects my best recollections of experiences that occurred over fifty years ago. I've changed some names and characteristics, compressed some events, and recreated some dialogue. The Camp Reasoner part of the Tun Tavern chapter is fictionalized but embodies the spirit of what went down at base camp during my time there.

PREFACE

> A hero is someone who has given his or her
> life to something bigger than oneself.
> — Joseph Campbell

When I returned from Vietnam in 1971, I didn't expect I'd be embraced with open arms as a public servant deserving praise. While in-country, we Marines heard plenty about the less-than-hospitable treatment returning soldiers received from segments of the American public. Part of me understood. It was a turbulent and controversial time.

I was coming home to Marin County, California, a predominately liberal community critical of the war. And while Marin culture was tolerant, spiritual, and forward-looking in many respects, I doubted I'd get a free pass as a homegrown guy who spent a year of his young life in the jungles and bush of Vietnam, despite my in-step political leanings.

I wasn't mistaken. Soon after landing on U.S. soil, I tasted the bitterness of what it was like being a Vietnam War veteran. It wasn't pretty.

While no one spit on me or called me a baby-killer, the mere mention of my Marine-war- veteran status offended people and killed conversations like a fly swatter on flies. I found it awkward interacting regularly with people who had for many months and even years passionately protested an image they had of someone like me. I realized that so long as I identified as a combat soldier, I'd be persona non grata in local social circles. If I wanted to get on with my life more smoothly, better that I live a kind of lie, constructing an image that excluded the recent past.

I effectively went underground as a veteran and adapted to the times. I grew my hair long, and, but for a few close friends, I avoided mentioning my Marine experience in Vietnam. It paid off. Keeping mum about my military past enhanced my social life, including romantically. I integrated more seamlessly. When asked about my background, I leapfrogged over what I did in uniform and moved conversations elsewhere. For me, what was past was past and not prologue.

Separated from military life, I began to explore different avenues to express myself and fill my potential. I threw myself into many pursuits, including as a locomotive engineer, fitness trainer, distance runner, professional gambler, Reiki practitioner, commercial diver, massage therapist, and tool-sharpening business operator. Despite wearing those many hats, however, I kept the boonie headgear I wore in Vietnam and other paraphernalia. I thought no one, including myself, would be the worse for wear being in the dark about my military experiences.

Then something unanticipated happened.

Gina, my wife, one of the few who knew about my military service, although not the less-than-savory details, decided to get informed about veterans benefits. She enlisted a high school running buddy of mine, Don Makela, who had corresponded with me while in Vietnam and had experience getting stuff from the military. Undertaking the project with their usual gusto, they obtained a mound of documentation from the government. As it turned out, the materials included something my wife hadn't anticipated—a war citation from the Department of the Navy (which includes the Marines). When I came home that night, Gina asked why I hadn't mentioned the citation all those years ago.

My response was simple: Citation? What citation? I had no clue the Navy had issued me a commendation. It was news to both of us. The citation concerned a skirmish in South Vietnam on June 19, 1970, during one of my many reconnaissance missions. I later learned the Marines had tried to find me without success, which was why, according to them, they'd never awarded me the accompanying medal. The citation reads in part:

> While walking in the dangerous point position during a seven-man reconnaissance patrol, [Corporal Walton] came into point-to-point contact with an enemy patrol. Reacting instantly, Corporal Walton opened fire at the enemy point man and killed him, and then as he attempted to fire at another hostile soldier, his rifle malfunctioned.
>
> Maintaining his composure, Corporal Walton immediately corrected the malfunction and killed the approaching enemy soldier. As a result of his heroic and timely actions, his team was extracted without further incident.

I had a foggy memory of this episode. Like most everything else regarding my time in Vietnam, my ability to recall had clotted into a tangled cluster of an entombed past. I had no reason to doubt it happened as described and every reason to assume it likely did. It spoke of reality. Still, I didn't pay the news much mind. *Terrific, but what are we doing for dinner?*

But matters weren't entirely in my control. The quest to identify veterans benefits led to my seeing a therapist to address the PTSD I'd carried inside, untouched for decades. During one of the earlier sessions, the therapist noticed the citation in my personnel file and took it upon himself to bring the matter to the attention of military brass. Shortly thereafter, I received a call from a Navy Captain who advised me the Department of the Navy wanted to hold a formal ceremony in the city of Novato (Marin County), my hometown, to award me the medal. It would be a public ceremony and might generate local media attention.

I resisted. I wanted that part of my life to remain hidden from the public eye and stay a personal matter. While acknowledgement was nice, even in a dusty stashed-away military file, I preferred my life as it was.

My wife, however, felt otherwise. She pointed out that family, friends, and the community deserved the chance to honor me for what I did and earned. I relented.

On June 13, 2012, the Marin County chapter of the Military Officer Association of America held a ceremony in Novato. To my astonishment, it was well attended. At the ceremony, Major Christopher Esrey, USMC, formally awarded me the Navy Commendation Medal with V for Valor. It was a humbling experience that compelled me to come to grips publicly with what I had avoided for over forty years. I was uncomfortable in the setting but appreciated and felt the warmth, gratitude, and love from everyone.

The news of my background as a Marine stunned friends and business associates. Not only had they no idea about my war involvement, but their images of a Marine veteran didn't fit how they saw me. When word spilled into the community, I received half-playful pushback for not previously sharing my military time and exploits and heard a litany of different versions of, "I'm your friend, your buddy, and you couldn't tell me about your past? What's up with that?"

I understood the reactions. But I also didn't feel shame or guilt. The decision I'd made many years prior to keeping things under wraps had served me well. Still, in fairness, that was then, and this was now. I was beginning to feel and see things differently.

The public exposure of my military past sent me down memory lane. At first, honestly, I struggled with the memories. They were painful, sometimes ugly, and not entirely welcome. But I persevered. I began to talk more about it, and to my encouragement, people wanted to listen. The process had a healing effect. I could see the importance of sharing some of what I'd experienced, and maybe more than some of it. As I became more attuned to the process, I felt a powerful urge to tell people the truth of what went down during my time in Vietnam. I didn't want to sensationalize. I wanted to tell what I knew and saw and what I had felt in those days, without embellishment or regret.

The more I revisited the past, the more grateful I felt, not only for being alive, but for those who made courageous and selfless sacrifices to benefit me. I began to feel a surge of compassion for combat colleagues, young boys like me, with whom I served side-by-side. So many of them, dead and alive, didn't get the recognition I was fortunate to get at the medal ceremony. To me, they were and remain the unsung heroes of the war. They cast self-interest aside to save others. They were the reason I've had the life I've led. I wanted to honor them.

This book became the natural next step, my small way to acknowledge and celebrate those who put themselves at risk for me. It is a way to share how their unconditional support and loyalty was how I survived the war.

My coauthor, also a veteran, and I wanted to tell the story through their eyes to the extent practical, and we set out to locate some of the Marines with whom I served. Fifty years after the fact, it wasn't easy. Time and personal need sullied memories; people have died since. and, in some cases, deep wounds eclipsed any willingness to mine the darkness of war experiences. It was an imperfect process, but we got there.

The story of how I experienced Vietnam follows.

Ready to Roll
(LZ 401, the Recon Landing Zone at base of Camp Reasoner)

GLOSSARY

AK-47. A semiautomatic and automatic assault rifle the North Vietnamese Army (NVA) and Viet Cong (VC) used in Vietnam, known for its popping sounds.

AN/PRC 25 and 77 Radio Sets. Manpacks, portable VHF FM combat-net radio transceivers used to provide short-range, two-way radiotelephone voice communication.

APO. Army Post Office used for mail to Vietnam.

asshole buddy. Someone assigned on patrol to inspect the buttocks of a fellow patrol member for leeches that may have penetrated the body during the night.

azimuth. A straight direction expressed from the southern or northern horizon.

bandoliers. Belts worn around the chest to store ammunition.

base camp. A semipermanent main encampment providing supplies, shelter, and communications near a unit's tactical area.

Bell An-1 Cobra. A single-engine attack helicopter.

bird or big bird. An aircraft, usually a helicopter.

bomb crater. A large hole in the ground created during bombings, which occurred with great frequency in Vietnam.

boonie or brush hat. Soft floppy hat in camouflage green, worn on reconnaissance missions.

Bouncing Betty. Antipersonnel mine that propelled an explosive charge upward and scattered shrapnel at waist level.

briefing. Preparation session for an upcoming mission. It typically included a review of the military goals, prior patrol reports, maps, landing zones for insertion and extraction, hot zones, terrain, and anticipated weather patterns. Included a specific mission order.

Bronco. Twin-turboprop light attack and observation aircraft (North American Rockwell OV-10), developed for combat, with a variation for jungle warfare and equipped with rockets and miniguns.

bug juice. Insect repellant.

C-4. A plastic, putty-textured explosive that burns like Sterno when lit and was used to heat C-rations in the field.

Camp Reasoner. Base camp for a reconnaissance battalion, named for Medal of Honor winner Lt. Frank Reasoner, killed in action on 12 July 1965.

CH-46. Helicopter powered by twin turboshaft engines and armed with two door-mounted machine guns. It was the primary U.S. Marine troop transport aircraft during the Vietnam War.

Charlie. Term Americans commonly used to describe a Viet Cong soldier.

Chase plane. An aircraft that follows another aircraft for various purposes, including safety and making real-time observations.

Chinook. CH-47 cargo helicopter, larger than the CH-46 chopper. Slang for helicopter.

claymore mine. Antipersonnel mine that, when detonated, propelled small steel cubes in a sixty-degree, fan-shaped pattern to a maximum distance of one hundred meters.

Cobra. A gunship helicopter armed with mini-guns, rockets, and machine guns.

C-rations. Canned meals for use in the field, usually consisting of a basic course: a can of fruit, a packet of dessert, a packet of powdered cocoa, sometimes a small pack of cigarettes, and two pieces of chewing gum. See also K-rations (below).

corpsman. A Navy medical person serving the Marine Corps, similar to an Army medic.

debriefing. A post-mission assessment of the conduct and results of a mission.

di di mau. Vietnamese slang for "go quickly" or as adapted in the field, "get the fuck out of here."

Dogpatch. Section of town just outside the west gate of Da Nang International, between places called Four Corners and Freedom Hill. It was where military personnel obtained supplies and partied, even though off-limits.

elephant grass. Tall, razor-edged, indigenous tropical plant found in the Vietnam Highlands.

entrenching tool. A military digging tool.

extraction. Planned or emergency withdrawal by helicopter of troops from an operational area.

fatigues. Standard combat uniform in green.

firefight. Close-range exchange of small arms fire with the enemy.

Gatling gun. A six-barreled machine gun with rotating barrels and a high rate of fire—two thousand to six thousand rounds per minute.

grunt.   Slang for an infantryman.

HAC.   Helicopter aircraft commander or pilot.

hooch.   A hut or simple dwelling.

HQ.   Headquarters.

humping.   Slogging through jungle terrain with a backpack.

immersion foot.   A condition developed after having feet submerged in water for a prolonged period, causing cracking and bleeding.

in-country.   In South Vietnam.

insertion.   To be deployed—dropped off—in a tactical area by a chopper.

intel.   Military Intelligence that selected and designed our recon missions.

jungle juice.   Bug repellant.

jungle rot.   A fungal infection caused by contact with moisture in Vietnam.

jungle utilities.   Tropical combat uniforms, a.k.a. jungle fatigues.

Ka-Bar.   The standard-issue combat knife for Marines.

kill zone.   The radius within which an explosive device can kill virtually all occupants on detonation.

klick.   Kilometer.

K-rations.   Separately boxed, ready-to-eat meals for breakfast, supper (lunch), and dinner. K-rations were large cans for unit-sized servings while C-Rations were packaged for individual-sized combat rations.

LP.   Listening post outside the perimeter (see below), typically manned by two or three men at night as an early warning system against attack.

LZ. A small temporary clearing that served as a landing zone for a chopper.

M16. The standard U.S. military rifle used in Vietnam beginning in 1966 and the successor to the M-14.

M79. Also known as the blooper or blooker, a single-barrel, break-action 40 mm shotgun-like weapon, that discharges spin-armed "balls" or small grenades.

medevac. Helicopter medical evacuation from the field.

mortars. Explosive and high-arching shells typically used for close fire support.

Navy Commendation Medal with V. Mid-level military decoration for sustained acts of heroism with valor.

NESTOR. A family of compatible, tactical, and wideband-secured voice systems the U.S. National Security Agency developed and deployed during the Vietnam War.

NVA. North Vietnamese Army.

OV-10. Twin-turboprop light attack and observation aircraft, a.k.a. Bronco.

Paddle boat. The call name or call sign for a recon unit.

Pal Joey. Call name or call sign for my recon unit.

poncho liner. The nylon insert of a military rain poncho, often used as a blanket.

patrol leader. The Marine in charge of the recon patrol who has the final word in the field.

perimeter. Outer limits of a military position, typically created by bodies or mortars.

point man. Also known as "the point," the first man in the column on a recon or combat patrol.

PTSD. Post-traumatic stress disorder—symptoms that manifest after experiencing psychologically traumatic events outside the range of normal human experience.

punji pit. A booby trap made from short, sharpened wooden sticks, placed upright in the ground and covered with natural surroundings to conceal what is in the ground.

Purple Foxes. A helicopter squadron deployed at Marble Mountain in Vietnam from 1967–1971 (HMM-364, Helicopter Marine Medium), whose motto, painted on the tail with a purple fox in white oval, was "Give a Shit."

rear echelon motherfuckers. A.k.a. REMFs, generally meant to describe noncombat personnel, e.g., those working office duty, but more commonly used acrimoniously to refer to high-ranking officers who sent others into dangerous situations at no risk to themselves.

recon. Also known as reconnaissance missions; patrols that went into the jungle to gather intelligence on enemy activity.

red alert. The most urgent form of warning.

Rock Ape. Also known as Batutut or Nguòi rùng, a baboon-like creature, standing about four feet tall, indigenous to the rain forests of Vietnam, with a penchant for throwing rocks, if threatened.

staging camp. An NVA base camp used to plan missions and assaults.

Swiss Saddle (aka Swiss Seat). A harness used to secure combat soldiers, attached to ladders unfurled by helicopters for insertion and extraction when landing was unfeasible.

tail-end Charlie. The last person in the patrol column.

triple-canopy jungle. Plants and trees growing at three levels: ground, intermediate, and high. The triple canopy could rise to 300 feet or more, often blocking all light from reaching the jungle floor.

UNF.   Ultra high radio frequency.

utilities.   Lightweight tropical fatigues.

VC.   Viet Cong, also known as the National Liberation Front, a mass political organization in South Vietnam with its own army—People›s Liberation Armed Forces of South Vietnam (PLAF)—that fought against the U.S. and South Vietnamese in the Vietnam War.

VNF.   Very high radio frequency.

wait-a-minute vines.   A prickly plant prevalent in Vietnam with sharp thorns that grabbed and cut clothes and body parts and often forced a stoppage in movement.

white phosphorus smoke grenade.   An aerial grenade that released a large puff of white smoke from hot phosphorus that burned on contact.

Wilson Pickett.   A.k.a. Willy Pete, slang for the white phosphorus smoke grenade.

The World.   The United States.

— 1 —

WAITING

> I think I'm afraid to be happy because whenever
> I get too happy, something bad happens.
> — Charlie Brown

I am sitting alone under a banyan tree in Vietnam. By myself. I like being alone. It minimizes reminders of war and makes me feel alive. It is the afternoon. Rain is falling lightly.

Sitting here, it is hard to fathom that death can come without a second's notice, thousands of miles from home, huddled under a poncho, the pitter-patter of raindrops hitting my camouflaged boonie headgear. I look up at the sky, barely visible, darkened not by night but by natural surroundings, the triple-canopy jungle and hovering gray clouds, my body shivering cold in scorching jungle temperatures, my depleted body a collection of filth, sores, bites, rashes, and other markings. I'm not sure what they are.

In the moment, I feel like a beaten-down young man, not even old enough to vote like most of the other Marines I am serving with, as I await my next rendezvous with the enemy, someone out there who wants to kill me, doesn't know me but wants to off me posthaste.

Death can literally come after my next breath. But the truth is that at some point, you don't give a shit. You truly don't give a shit. We are in this godforsaken war, and we either aren't getting out alive or well, that much you can book. Death, mutilated, or soulless. Roll the dice.

It keeps raining. The sun is hidden. I command it in my mind: *Sun, show yourself.* You keep zapping my energy, dehydrating my body. The least you can do is show yourself.

After a while, sitting under that banyan tree, I get comfortable, all the discomfort becoming normalized, and my mind wanders away from the jungle, away from war. I think of home, the spectacular beauty of Marin County, the many hills I've run there, the many people I've run with, and all the youthful partying. Sweet times then, memories now.

I think of girlfriends and the good times we had. The reminiscing reminds me that in my pocket, folded into a nice square, is a letter from one of them. I take it out to read and quickly realize I've read this one probably five times. I have to do a better job at recycling the many letters I get. I need a system. Still, I read this one again, and it makes me smile, something I am reminded of that I've not done in the past several weeks, and that saddens me, and I long for home.

But I can't spend time in the black hole of wishful thinking. I know where I am and will be for many more months—if I am lucky. I know too that the next day I have another recon mission, another excursion into the jungle in search of information to advance the war effort, or maybe to capture a targeted enemy officer to bring back for interrogation, an even more dangerous assignment as it requires penetrating an enemy base camp.

I wonder about these missions, how well HQ intelligence thinks them through, how much they handicap our chances of success balanced against the risks we face. Do they even assess the risks from the comfy confines of their HQ offices? Is that a factor in deciding to send us out? We never know these things. We get the HQ mandate, prepare as well as we can, and get on with it. Doubt and resentment can't factor into the equation. We all depend on each other. We all must trust each other.

But if truth be known, sitting under that tree, cold and dirty, depleted and forlorn, I harbor some resentment. I despise officers, nothing personal, mind you, more the bars on their shoulders. I don't like being under their thumb all the time, and I sure as hell don't like some of the missions they send us on, full of doomsday strategy from the start. But they are the cards we recon Marines are dealt. We follow orders religiously.

Yeah, Jesus, I am in a war zone. How the hell did that happen? Not too long ago I was a student at the College of Marin learning about science, the environment, and literature, a veritable deep exploration into the wonders of life.

Now I am in Vietnam learning how to kill and how not to be killed.

One step forward . . .

Each day is the worst day. I can die today and it's over. Each day is the best day. I am alive again and can hope for tomorrow.

It gets quiet suddenly. The winds slow. The large leathery leaves of the banyan tree get still, save droplets of water easing off their tips like molasses.

In my prior life, quiet was good, a peaceful interlude to chill and absorb the beauty of the world. Now it is scary as hell, possessing all the earmarks of imminent death. You know what they say. You'll never hear what hits you. Those you leave behind to fight the good fight, they will hear the noise that kills you. They will remember it forever, even if you fade from their memories.

In the stillness of the air, I can feel what is happening to me. This place is destroying part of my heart and digging a hole in my soul. Down deep, I know I will never be the same. Who would if you think about it? We see maimed and dead people all the time. We suffer small doses of fear virtually each day. And we kill. Together we take the lives of others we don't know and will never know because we are told to do so for some cause we don't quite understand or give a shit about and will never embrace. How could anyone survive all that intact? I know who I was before this. I don't know how different I am now, and I certainly don't know what I will become, assuming I become.

Measured in emotional years, how old will I be when I return?

I am cool with losing some of this time in my life. I hopefully will have many chances ahead to make up for it. I am not so cool with losing who I was and years of my psychic development. I was a happy-go-lucky kid when I became a Marine. Always smiling. Always joking. Always loving life. Will that splendid spirit and humor drain out of me during my tour? That prospect scares the hell out of me.

I confess to getting angry sometimes. I get angry when an assigned mission strikes me as insane. I get angry when one of ours is killed, worse if I knew him. I get angry at myself for putting me in this situation. I get angry at the powers that be for not ending this reckless war. I get angry at the world for all the wars it has allowed. I get angry because it sometimes feels good to be angry, gives me moral and emotional ballast.

I wonder, though, what will happen with all that anger when I return to The World. Will it get discharged like I get discharged from the Corps? Will it linger and make constant cameo appearances in my life? Don't know. Hope I live to find out.

The rain has eased up. I see in the distance a narrow swath of blue. I don't want to get up. I like this tree. It enlivens me a little. I want to take it all in. I want to feel what it is like to still be alive. Tomorrow can wait.

RECONNAISSANCE

> Military intelligence is the key to war;
> without it, you cannot win.
>
> — Sun Tzu

Reconnaissance work in Vietnam, at its most basic level, was designed to generate military intelligence. The idea was straightforward: military brass dispatched a patrol team six or seven strong deep into enemy territory with specific intelligence directives. The assignment might, for example, entail observing tangible structures, identifying enemy supply routes or encampments, deconstructing recent enemy movement, or the most common for my patrol teams, kidnapping high-ranking officers.

Once we completed the mission, with info or prisoner in hand, we were not to dally but to return to base camp with urgency and, hopefully, minimal difficulty. Upon arrival at base camp, we got debriefed and, hopefully as well, commended on a job well done. We'd have a few days to rest before the next mission.

Our missions were not designed to engage the enemy. We were not, technically speaking, combat soldiers on a search and destroy mission. Our jobs were more narrowly defined. We were gatherers not hunters. And lest there be any doubt, that is how we were equipped. We brought enough weaponry to defend and push back, but if we found ourselves in a prolonged battle, we'd likely be in deep trouble. We couldn't handle a sustained fight without artillery or other assistance. We lacked the firepower.

As you might imagine, our nonengagement mandate didn't always work out as designed. The enemy never got those memos.

We were special forces, performing unconventional military operations. That meant we were specially and vigorously trained for recon both stateside and in-country. Normally, recon training was a two-year program. Sometimes, however, Marines, like me, were pressed into service on an expedited immersion basis because of the diminishing supply of recon personnel. The realities of jungle warfare often sidelined the well-intentioned rules and protocols the military crafted for the Vietnam War. U.S. military forces had limited historical experience fighting in jungles and navigating rainforests, meaning a steep on-the-job learning curve. It also meant we had to devise solutions on the fly, adapting to an unfamiliar situation with moving targets. To keep step with the pace of war, we had to adjust. A lot.

Don't misunderstand. My less than two-year recon training was difficult. It included a long list of exhausting activities, including helicopter rope suspension training, small unit tactics, advance patrolling, training in obstacle clearing for landing zone preparation, radio communication, rappelling from hovering helicopters, advanced land navigation, dropping from sixty feet on a rope, surveillance techniques, in-depth reading of maps and the compass, use of explosives, including C-4 cartridges and claymore mines, training in weapons like the .45 pistol and the M79 grenade launcher, and mind-breaking conditioning work on land and in water. Most of the physical training included sixty-pound packs on our backs. It was brutal.

Training How to Rappel

Before landing in Vietnam, I was a long-distance runner. I competed at a high level, and when I became a Marine, I presumed I was in top condition. I learned painfully and quickly that I didn't know what top conditioning meant. The Marine trainers worked us to the bone. They tested the boundaries of individual physical and mental tolerance. They challenged us to find human gears we didn't know existed and mental stamina we couldn't imagine ever having.

Marine leadership knew how to get us physically ready for what we were about to face. Emotional readiness, well, that was an entirely different matter. That would come with time, assuming time was kind to us. But so far as physicality and mental prowess were concerned, when we got assigned recon work, when those missions started coming our way, and we got thrust deep into the morass of the jungle, we were as ready as ready could be.

We had no say in the missions our superiors crafted for us. Sometimes the thinking behind them puzzled us and seemed unnecessarily dangerous for a questionable return. But in the words of Alfred, Lord Tennyson, in his epic poem, *The Charge of the Light Brigade*, about soldiers fighting in the Crimean War, "Theirs not to reason why, theirs but to do or die." Mr. Tennyson understood recon Marines before their time. And so, we did what we were charged with doing, no matter how headshaking the assignment.

The Marine Corps is a separate military service within the Department of the Navy. It assigns forces and units to combatant commands globally. During the Vietnam War, the Marine Corps units were assigned to MAC-V (Military Assistance Command-Vietnam). Before each mission, Intel briefed the patrol leader and assistant patrol leader on our orders. I, at different times, functioned in both roles and attended my share of briefings. They were focused and intense.

During the briefing sessions, we reviewed prior patrol reports that contained intelligence relevant to the new mission, examined maps and characteristics of the terrain we anticipated humping, pinpointed and evaluated the selected insertion site—where we'd get deposited by helicopter—and the selected extraction site—where we'd get picked up to return to base camp. We also identified likely "hot zones" to avoid, assessed weather forecasts, as well as a host of other details that we needed to master.

It was understood and expected that attention to detail was not only important, as might be expected, but essential. We were repeatedly told—to state the obvious—that precision in execution, from top to bottom, could be what determined a successful or failed mission and whether we lived or died or survived less than whole. Punches didn't get pulled. Shortcuts weren't tolerated (more on that later).

Before boarding the helicopter en route to a mission, we were expected to examine what we were bringing at least twice, in painstaking detail, reflecting the specific circumstances of the mission, to assure everything was in working order, from weaponry and clothing to insect repellant and food and water supplies. We left nothing to chance within our control, looking ahead as best we could. The jungle and the enemy had more than ample capacity to spring surprises on us. We could ill afford to spring any on ourselves. We had to be as prepared as we could for whatever we expected and—as strange as it sounds—for the unexpected. It was diligent preparation to a fault.

The Marines, it is often said, have a cult quality. Therein lies a basic truth. Marine identity and affiliation transcend time in service. The bonds between Marines are perpetual. It is not surprising that Marine recon had a subculture, shaped by a family mentality with bonds that grew tighter and stronger with each mission.

This is the Marine RECON creed:

Realizing it is my choice and my choice alone to be a Reconnaissance Marine, I accept all challenges involved with this profession. Forever shall I strive to maintain the tremendous reputation of those who went before me.

Exceeding beyond the limitations set down by others shall be my goal. Sacrificing personal comforts and dedicating myself to the completion of the reconnaissance mission shall be my life. Physical fitness, mental attitude, and high ethics—The title of Recon Marine is my honor.

Conquering all obstacles, both large and small, I shall never quit. To quit, to surrender, to give up is to fail. To be a Recon Marine is to surpass failure, to overcome, to adapt and to do whatever it takes to complete the mission.

On the battlefield, as in all areas of life, I shall stand tall above the competition. Through professional pride, integrity, and teamwork, I shall be the example for all Marines to emulate.

Never shall I forget the principles I accepted to become a Recon Marine. Honor, Perseverance, Spirit and Heart. A Recon Marine can speak without saying a word and achieve what others can only imagine.

The one constant in my Marine reconnaissance experience, the thing I will never forget and for which I will be forever grateful, was the loyalty patrol members had for one another. I never for a moment felt I couldn't rely on everyone in my patrol team. I knew that if the shit ever hit the fan—and hit the fan it did—each of my fellow team members would have my back. Each would risk his life to save mine. It didn't matter if we were friends or even liked each other or whether our backgrounds or religious bearings meshed or conflicted. None of that mattered. We had a bond specific to our circumstance, a connection that kept us hitched to each other, in the constant quest for survival. It was brotherhood in the purest sense of the word.

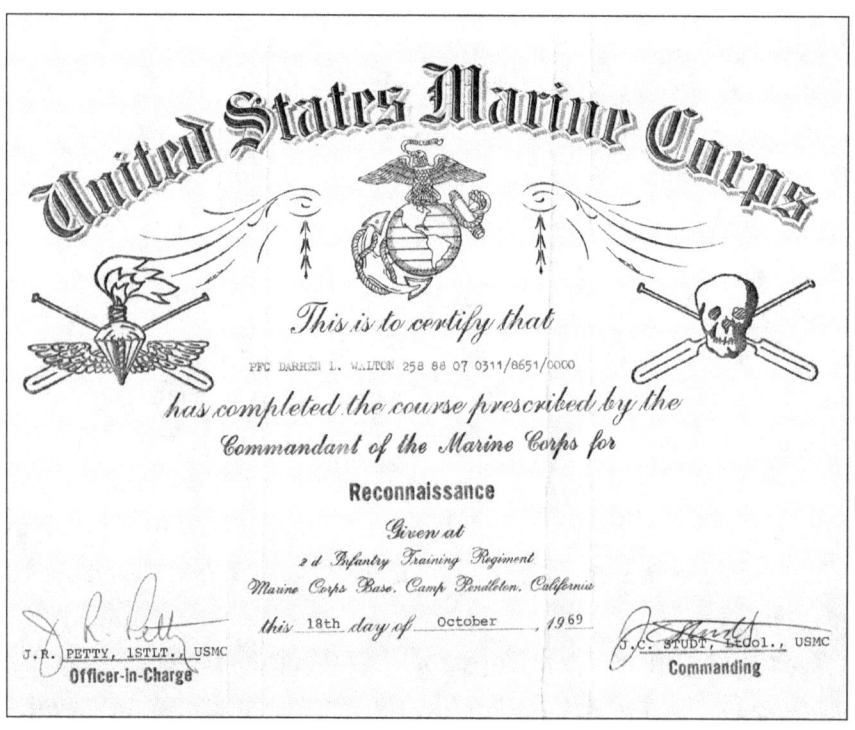

⇒ 3 ⇐

CAMP REASONER

Greater Love Hath No Man
—Stone etching honoring fallen Marine
Lt. Frank Reasoner

C amp Reasoner was the base camp for my reconnaissance
work in Vietnam, my cherished home away from home. It
was where everything started for us recon Marines and, if
we were lucky, in the cycle of our work, where everything would
end. We hauled our butts on one surveillance mission after the
other, back and forth from the jungle, for months on end.

The name of the camp is a dedication to Marine 1st Lt. Frank
Reasoner, whom the Marines posthumously awarded the first-
ever Medal of Honor during the Vietnam War. Lt. Reasoner was
a classic military hero. In July 1965, his eighteen-man patrol operating southwest of Da Nang had deeply penetrated enemy-controlled territory and got ambushed by a Viet Cong (VC) compa-
ny-sized force. The superior enemy numbers and the advantage
of surprise allowed the VC to launch a vicious and relentless attack against the unsuspecting Marines from several concealed
positions. Lt. Reasoner isolated himself from the main body of
his unit to organize a base of fire for a response, putting himself
at grave risk. The firepower of the enemy, however, prevented

his unit from moving forward, forcing him to provide cover for his men with his weapon, repeatedly exposing himself to a torrent of enemy fire. As casualties mounted, he ran to the aid of a wounded radioman, and as he did, took a blast of fire that killed him. Lt. Reasoner was twenty-seven years old.

Camp Reasoner was located several miles southwest of Da Nang on a sprawling piece of arid land sometimes referred to as Hill 327. It was pitched on a slope of a high-rising hill at the edge of a large collection of old rice paddies. Its perimeter was wrapped in barbed wire. It had a safe and advantageous location with sentry entry points.

Inside the protected exterior was a series of buildings, most notably battalion headquarters and an operations center for senior military leadership; dozens of SEA (Southeast Asia) huts made of corrugated metal, or hooches as we called them, with their rudimentary cots inside; and a surprisingly well-stocked mess hall with cold and hot food, as well as tables with tablecloths.

For me, at least, the hooches, which I shared typically with about six Marines at any given time, were my favorite place in the camp. Despite the comings and goings of fellow Marine housemates, the hooch was the closest we'd ever come to a private space for alone time. It was truly a sanctuary, makeshift, mind you, but a sanctuary, nevertheless.

We also had a universal shower, functionally speaking. It came courtesy of a water tank that military personnel before us had inserted on a hill behind the combat base with a feed pipe that delivered water downhill to waiting camouflaged-faced, dirty, and smelly Marines. The water tank was fixed about two hundred feet up the hill, an elevation that generally guaranteed good water pressure. The water temperature, however, was naturally cold at best, save when the sun heated the tank sufficiently to raise the temperature to almost normal levels. The vacillating water temperatures encouraged late afternoon visits to the shower on non-monsoon days. But cold or hot, nobody cared. A shower was a shower no matter what the water temperature.

The pulse of Camp Reasoner was its LZ, the place from which helicopters took off and landed. The LZ at Reasoner was once a rough-surfaced dirt patch, punctuated by a light-bulb- filled tin can jammed into the ground for nighttime landings. It was a primitive arrangement in the early days with limited chopper capacity, able to accommodate but a few at a time.

By the time I arrived there, though, after the war had escalated exponentially, senior military leadership had expanded the LZ and paved it with asphalt, allowing it to accommodate about ten to twelve choppers. Serious business.

The Reasoner LZ may not have been anything to look at, unless military helicopters fascinated you. But despite its barren, metallic look, it was hallowed ground, an outdoor temple that held the power of the full range of wartime emotions.

When it served as the site of our departures, lifting us skyward en route to a mission and the jungle insertion, it became a source of anxiety, thrill, and fear, where any second thoughts you may have had about what you signed up for were too little, too late. We were headed into danger, and there was no turning back. As we rose from the ground, higher and higher, the comfy confines of Camp Reasoner faded from view, and we knew but never said, maybe forever. We each entered the clouds with our private thoughts, revealing nothing.

In contrast, after a completed mission, we descended toward the asphalt, all of us melded into one large psychic exhale. It brought muted happiness and genuine appreciation for the luck or divine intervention that spared your ass and gifted you the chance to sleep under cover from the elements and enjoy a shower and warm meal. You would live another day.

The LZ became the barometer for everything we felt deeply about the war.

* * *

Camp Reasoner had two enlisted clubs. One, Wynn Hall, named after Lance Corporal Joseph R. Wynn, was also called the Battalion Beer Garden. Wynn was a recon Marine rifleman from Georgia who was killed in Quang Nam province in May 1965 while on a recon mission with the Third Recon Battalion, which occupied Camp Reasoner before my battalion, the First Recon Battalion, claimed it as home. Small arms fire felled him while with his recon patrol team, the first member of his company (D) to lose his life. He was eighteen.

Wynn Hall had a concrete floor, bamboo support poles, and a thatched roof, a design that would never be the envy of elite social clubs in Manhattan. But it was sturdy and served its purpose. Outside the club were several tables and chairs strewn about with shifting locations, depending on group energy, to simulate an active small bar where we imbibed beer and soda. It became a place to let your hair down, such as we had, a place to forget where we were, if that were possible.

The other facility, primarily available for us non-officer types, was the Staggerback Inn, described in Chapter 10 (Tun Tavern).

THE BUNKERS

Camp Reasoner also had various bunkers.

The slit trench. Outside each hut, we built a slit trench—essentially a long foxhole—bordered by sandbags on each side. Slit trenches were three feet wide and two-and-a-half feet deep. If the shit hit the fan, we would all haul ass and pile into the trenches end to end. They were relatively safe places during any aerial attack, reliable protection against shrapnel. It would take a direct hit to kill any of us. At night, if you lost track of where the trenches were, or had that extra beer you swore you shouldn't have, you could easily fall into them.

Ammo bunkers. Reasoner also had an ammo bunker dug into the side of a hill across from the LZ. The front displayed a double layer of sandbag walls in an L-shape that led to the door. The sandbag structure prevented a direct enemy hit from nearby launch locations. Inside the maze of sandbags was a door behind which we would go to get our ammo. On the side of the hill hung a red sign that said, "No Smoking." For real.

Adjacent to the bunker were two fifty-five-gallon drums turned sideways, put into the side of the mountain, half filled with sand. Before a patrol, our patrol leader would assemble the team and direct us to hit the ammo bunker for ammo, radio, and batteries, among other stored items needed on a patrol. When we returned from patrol, we had to empty our weapons of ammo into those drums and pull the trigger to confirm the cleared weapon.

The S3 bunker (current operations). The S3 bunker was the big enchilada for operations. It was not the kind of place open for general admission. To get there, you took a dirt trail from the landing zone that wound up the hill directly above the LZ. On arrival you faced a triple-sandbagged front with big beams that framed a wooden door, like a coal mine shaft with an entrance hallway. Entering, you found yourself in a foyer that had pegs installed on a four-by-eight railroad tie fixed to the bunker wall for hanging rifles, assuming you were permitted to enter. Also on the railroad tie was a red light above the bulkhead. If a recon patrol team was in contact with S3 operations during a mission, the red light got flipped on, signaling a command of silence in the bunker and a prohibition to enter, unless specifically invited.

Beyond the foyer were three rooms. One was private work-space for the S3 major with a drape across the entry. No one went in there generally except to bring the major chow. He had a cot or a bed and a desk and often slept there. He essentially lived in the bunker.

The second was the main operations room, open in the center, containing both map and clipboard walls. It was huge, over 400 square feet. The right wall displayed a floor-to-ceiling twelve-foot group of maps, one laid on top of the other, featuring various areas in operation, with plastic, see-through acetate roll-up charts that when rolled down showed the recon zones with specific information. Each map could be dropped down to show distinct aspects of the landscape and terrain. You could roll down one map to see the hashtags that lined up with the grids. Each layer had its own data that, while historic, provided critical insight.

For example, the booby trap map included all the areas where booby traps had been determined to be in areas of operation. It might include a cluster of booby traps around a village, which meant that the vicinity likely housed a bomb maker and where the enemy could be assumed to have installed new booby traps near the village, not currently detected on the map.

The clipboard wall contained clipboards with a source of current patrol operations. Every team had its own clipboard. It contained a roster of those on patrol, their weapons identified with serial numbers, the relevant warning order (which identified the mission), and a fragmentation ("frag") order (which identified the plan). And, equally important, whenever the patrol made contact, the communication guys, in the third bunker room (see below), recorded records of all incoming information onto the clipboard to allow operations to keep track of what was happening during a mission.

The third room was a radio room with built-in benches for the radio operators on duty. It was about eight feet deep and twenty-one feet across. There were always four radio operators and a radio chief on duty, manning all the radios, which constantly received communications from the field. The operators transmitted what they heard to the radio chief, who, after review, initialed the data and transmitted the information to the S3 chief on watch, who in turn reviewed and initialed it before transmitting it to the watch officer, an experienced first lieutenant who also initialed it before the information found its way to the clipboard.

On the backside, in the middle of the room, was a dugout with two desks, one for the S3 alpha, the senior first lieutenant, and the other for the master sergeant who functioned as operations chief. The master sergeant's job was to oversee the operations center. There was a side office to the right for two officers using plywood desks. One was the air liaison officer from the air wing whose full-time job was inserting and extracting packages. The other was the liaison officer from the artillery regiment who was responsible for artillery support.

At the end of the patrol, camp military intelligence—the lieutenant colonel commander, the S3 major, the watch officer, and watch non-commissioned officer—reviewed the information on the clipboard in the S2 shop (two Southeast Asian huts). Typically, the debriefings included the patrol leader and assistant patrol leader from the recon unit, although they could expand to include other members or even the entire team if significant activity occurred. For members of the patrol, the clipboard during the debriefing functioned as a memory jogger, sometimes with as many as twenty spot reports, chronologically listed, over the course of several days in the field.

The goal of the debriefing was to garner as much knowledge as possible to create a reliable permanent record of what happened on the patrol. Normally, the discussion tracked and reaffirmed what was on the clipboard. Sometimes, added information arose from follow-up questions, for example, What was the NVA wearing? Which direction did they go? How many did you see? What were they carrying? When did you hear them? Sometimes, there were differing perspectives on what occurred during a firefight; this was a natural occurrence, no rights or wrongs, only separate ways of experiencing the same harrowing event.

After the debriefing, we would leave and grab a shower, head to the club, and have a beer and a meal. If there was a question about any judgment call, we would be called in, usually after we rested, sometimes that evening, but most of the time the next day, over a cup of coffee by somebody senior looking for clarification, especially if things had gotten hairy on the patrol, forcing spontaneous decision-making.

Here is an example of how a judgment call was handled:

While on a recon patrol, a unit found a baby, still alive, after a firefight and after the NVA had left the area. Concerned for the life of the baby, and the mission still in full swing, the patrol leader requested that the S3 major back at Camp Reasoner authorize an immediate extraction of the child. The S3 major, however, refused, ordering the patrol leader to leave the baby and continue with the mission. If it had been a POW, no doubt S3 would not have blinked and dispatched an emergency extraction forthwith.

The patrol leader made the humanitarian election to override the order. He kept the baby with the unit, feeding it sugar water for three days, keeping it alive. The unit eventually made its way to the initially planned extraction site.

Once airborne in the chopper, the patrol leader directed the pilot to make an interim landing at a medical facility, where he disembarked and brought the baby to the emergency room and bolted, leaving the child in the good hands of hospital personnel. The child survived.

When the patrol leader returned, after the customary S2 debriefing, in a subsequent meeting, he received a dressing down by his company commander for refusing to honor a direct order. The colonel, however, knew two things in conflict: he had to back his major—that is how it is done in the U.S. Marine Corps—and the major erred giving the order. He transferred the patrol leader from Recon Battalion to First Force Recon, a mild reprimand, working for a different commander in a different place, where he continued to flourish as a team leader in Marine reconnaissance.

More on judgment calls in Chapter 11 (The Decision).

The machine gun bunker (Post 4). This bunker had four pillars in the form of railroad ties, sandbagged on three sides, with a sandbag roof, housing an M60 machine gun that peered over the rice paddies in the eastern sector of the base.

DOGPATCH

Near Camp Reasoner was the village of Dogpatch, strategically located for trade because of its proximity to Freedom Hill. Dogpatch was off-limits to the Marines, which meant it was a magnet for exploration. On occasion, we'd sneak off base to visit a popular, skanky, old bar in Dogpatch, packing loaded .45 sidearms as a precaution. We did not carry rifles into Dogpatch. It was rumored that deeper down the road we might find brothels, massage parlors, and dope dealers peddling their wares. I stayed clear of all that, as did my fellow recon members, but I wouldn't doubt for a second that all kinds of sordid activity went down nearby. War can incite an irresistible hunger for many things considered verboten.

Instead, my buddies and I hung out at the bar in peaceful co-existence with whomever was there, not always Americans, our own demilitarized zone, everyone friendly, buying each other drinks. Of course, it probably would not have taken much to upset the fragile equanimity. Despite the harmless haven of the bar, tensions still percolated inside each of us. One wrong word or leer could flip the switch, triggering bedlam.

Dogpatch represented a few hours of unapproved breaks in the action, a respite from madness, a brief flirtation with what awaited us at home, should we make it back. What went down there was hardly a secret but it was better left unsaid. Even the hardest of the brass hardliners allowed relief valves. The alternative might have been insanity.

* * *

MAIL

A couple of days a week, we had mail call. Those of us on base—the others typically were on a mission—would collect at a specific spot in the late afternoon to get our mail. The person in charge would haul a large gunny sack, bulging at the sides, and everyone would surround him in a semicircle. Piece by piece, letters and packages, he'd locate the name and address and call it out, a ritual that continued until that sack deflated to nothing.

I was blessed. I received mail often: family care packages, letters from lady friends, letters and care packages from neighbors, especially mothers. I always had somebody, maybe not on a regular basis, but I always had something. One girlfriend liked to send me a perfumed letter and envelope, which my fellow Marines loved to whiff. I'd often take pieces of mail on missions. It'd be something to read, over and over, and provide splotches of optimism, help you in the quest to stay sane. I relied heavily on the mail for my emotional well-being, my stable state of mind.

Receiving mail is what hope was all about, generating feelings of love and caring, knowing you had not been forgotten and, better still, were missed, maintaining bonds, and overall, getting a boost to your constantly plummeting morale. Military mail was a lifeline.

Mail could be intensely private. On occasion, a Marine would take a letter to a place where he'd have privacy, like behind a large rock or an imposing tree. Every now and then, you'd hear a badass recon Marine bawling his eyes out as he read the letter. You didn't know if they were happy or sad tears, only that the letter meant a lot and triggered powerful feelings.

But not everyone got mail each gathering or each week, and some folks almost never got mail. That saddened me deeply. I'd pay special attention to those Marines, make sure they were respected and loved and much appreciated.

* * *

Camp Reasoner was my home for one year, the beginning and end spot for everything I did as a recon Marine. It was where I stayed when not on patrol in the jungle and where I couldn't wait to get back to once we ventured into the jungle for missions. We filled our time between each mission in various ways: reading, writing letters, sharing photos, telling stories about life back in The World, and mindlessly shooting the shit to avoid obsessing about how many days we had left in-country. The days and nights spent at Camp Reasoner, removed from the jungle trails and all that entailed, were peaceful, quiet, and, not insignificantly, relatively safe. That counted for a lot, given the alternative.

I can still visualize Camp Reasoner. I can still smell its scents and hear its noises and see its rising suns and sweeping views. I don't miss the place. But it has an important place in my history and that of so many Marines. I am grateful for what it became for me, a shelter from formidable natural and enemy forces and a haven from sheer madness.

Camp Reasoner 1970

Camp Reasoner Circa 2019

THE TEAM

> Alone we can do so little; together
> we can do so much.
>
> — Helen Keller

The first lesson of boot camp came courtesy of the ceremonial shaving of heads. It was more than a demonstration of who's boss, an emasculation that emphasized our inferior military standing. It announced a rite of passage, an introduction to a new persona we were expected to become and embrace—without challenge or deviation.

The Marine Corps had no place for civilian habits, claims to fame, and titles. When we joined the cult, the person we knew as ourselves died, and another entirely new identity, a one-for-all, all-for-one, battle-ready Marine took its place. It was a resurrection, military style, with slavish adherence to rules and orders. From a military perspective, it was the purest form of what being part of a team meant.

In combat, each team member had a designated role to perform. We were told repeatedly, and would learn, that the success of each military mission—and our lives—depended on precise execution of what we were taught and unbending compliance with what we were commanded to do. Going it alone put others at risk and undermined military tactics. We had to learn to trust each other with the ultimate gift—life—and be prepared to do what we could to live another day and, eventually, go home.

This principle had no clearer application than in reconnaissance work. Our recon unit was a small ensemble of young Marines, some still in their teens, each assigned and playing a different role, each dependent on the other, each committed to discharging their responsibilities to maximize the success on every mission, however defined. It didn't take long to develop camaraderie, more out of need and base instincts than natural cohesion or personal affinity. We were duty bound to support each other no matter what part of the country we came from, no matter what the color of our skin, no matter what our politics or religion. We suspended all differences for the common goal of survival—and completion of the mission. While that strong bond might have been temporary, limited to the imperatives of war, it was real, it was powerful, and it was invigorating.

Because survival required that we often communicate without words, we had to *sense* what each of us was thinking. We were inseparably bound in destiny, life or death. We were seven strong: point man, patrol leader, primary radioman, rifleman, secondary radioman, corpsman, and tail-end Charlie.

Point man. As the person at the front of the pack, the point man carried a weighty responsibility. He constantly looked to detect danger in immediate surroundings. The balance of the unit relied on him to do his job with utmost competence and vigilance. He couldn't let his comrades down, and, for that matter, their loved ones. A single mistake, a mere lapse, could doom them all.

The point sometimes doubled as assistant patrol leader, ready to take command should something happen to the patrol leader, in which case someone else assumed the point position.

The point's main role required a talent that couldn't be taught: a sixth sense for something amiss, irregularities on the trail that suggested trouble. The point man moved with keen caution, armed with a heightened sense for what may be out there, something that smell, hearing, or sight couldn't detect. His range of vision covered what was nearby—and immediate—primarily on the ground, like unnatural disturbances of the jungle floor, for example, trip wires, booby traps, and punji pits.

Punji pits deserve special mention. They were the most common trap in our field of operation—and the most lethal and disruptive. Punji pits, a hole a few feet deep and wide, bristled at the bottom with sharpened bamboo stakes that could penetrate clothing and the body like a steel knife. The enemy concealed them with a lattice of twigs, leaves, brush, or other overgrowth to harmonize with the natural landscape. If stepped on, the camouflage cover gave way, propelling the victim with the gravity of his own weight to the bottom of the pit where a formation of carefully stacked punji sticks tore flesh and ripped into muscle. The bamboo stakes were often bathed with feces or urine to increase chances of serious infection. A punji pit incident brought chaos and medical attention, distracting and depleting the ranks, and aiding an impending ambush. The point man was always the first at risk of this catastrophic happening.

While the point man often endured powerful adrenaline rushes, he had to maintain focus. He had to be on constant alert, *never* out of the moment, always dialed in to whatever might be out there, any minor thing that might make a difference in whether someone lived or died. He couldn't dwell on the magnitude of that responsibility or fall to the temptation to daydream, thinking about a loved one, the last letter from home he read, or what might await him if he survived to make it back to The World. For him, when on the trail, yesterday or tomorrow didn't exist, only the now. We measured life in fractions of seconds.

Patrol leader. The second man on the trail, the patrol leader, wore many hats. Foremost, he was the leader of the unit, the head honcho and alpha male, where the buck stopped. When push came to shove, what he said went. Commonly a sergeant, sometimes a corporal, the patrol leader was expected to have an unyielding commitment and loyalty to the recon unit, making decisions that protected each member within the parameters of the mission.

The patrol leader was charged with getting the mission prepared. He studied the details of the assigned missions, pouring over relevant reports on prior enemy sightings and base camps, firefights, and other potential hot spots. He learned with exacting precision the map coordinates, what trails to avoid, and which were safest. He inspected the patrol equipment to assure working order, checking more than once. He inventoried all our carry to make sure the unit had water and food for the specified duration of the patrol, commonly six days and nights, but no more to avoid an unnecessary load. Each part of the preparation was carefully handled, everything in strict order, to avoid mistakes. Precision reigned.

When the big birds inserted a recon unit onto the jungle floor, the patrol leader was expected to calm the nerves of his unit as they braced for the start of their mission. Dropping out of the chopper could expose the men to hostile fire, especially whenever the choppers struggled to find a relatively safe spot to disembark its eager passengers. And as his men disembarked, the patrol leader had to get them steely focused, despite the lingering sound of the chopper rotor blades fading in the distance, reminding them of what they knew, that their passage to safety was gone, and they were alone in the jungle.

The patrol leader was a navigator. He had to make sure the trails his unit humped were calculated to achieve mission goals in the safest way possible. He had to ensure his team stayed together, often a major challenge due to poor visibility in the triple-canopy jungle with everyone communicating with hand and body signals.

He had to be an evaluator of personnel, monitoring each of his men for signs of emotional, mental, or physical lapses or weaknesses. The pressure could be paralyzing, and a recon unit could get compromised if anyone tended to panic, lose focus, or allow fear to grip them by, for example, missing or misreading hand signals.

The same applied to conditioning. Recon work was physically grueling. Passing recon training, which as one patrol leader put it, was "the hardest, most physical demanding thing I ever had to go through in my life," didn't guarantee holding up in the jungle. The debilitating beatdown of the jungle experience could weaken those otherwise presumed strong, and the patrol leader had to head off any collapse as soon as he detected a mounting risk.

The patrol leader had to be an effective teacher. He had to ensure that his men knew how to deal with pressure. He taught them how to stifle coughs and practice silence using breathing techniques and the power of the mind to achieve a Buddha-like stillness, knowing there might be times the enemy was but several feet away in the bush, unaware of our presence. He taught them how to become invisible, including eliminating anything on their clothes that could sparkle in the sun and betray location. He taught them how to dissect sounds amid the deep blackness of the night to avoid panic. Was it an animal, an insect, the wind, or, more ominously, something that demanded immediate attention? He taught them how to do what he did, read a compass and a map, how to traverse ridges and elevation, understand coordinates, and communicate with hand signals and subtle head, eye, and arm movements. He taught these things to keep them alive and to make him replaceable if he went down.

Patrol leaders and point men worked in tandem, constantly in nonverbal communication. While the point man focused on immediate and close-range risks on the trail, eyes mostly downward, the patrol leader scanned over the top of the point man and down the road, looking for impending danger like a sniper, ambush, nearby enemy patrol, or base camp. They were four eyes and two sensory systems working as one with different but harmonized lines of vision.

In the final analysis, the patrol leader was the ultimate bodyguard, keeping his men constantly under his wing and demanding they listen to his commands with unyielding attention. His men might not always agree with him, but they had to trust his judgment and follow his lead. He commanded their respect. Like the point man, he could ill afford a mistake, as even a slight error could spell catastrophe. Above all, a personal mission proudly drove patrol leaders: that each of his unit survived to live in The World.

Primary radioman. The primary radioman was next in line behind the patrol leader with substantial control over the fate of the unit. Simply stated, the radioman was there to send and receive messages, to establish contact with others in the rear, either at base camp, headquarters, or in the air. He was the lifeline to help, reporting conflicts, firefights, or other enemy exchanges. The radioman called in medevacs, worked with the patrol leader to call in artillery strikes, and coordinated with pilots for extractions, helping to mark the LZ.

It was an unenviable role. Radiomen were exposed like no other. Whether they used the lighter three-foot antenna thrust above the head into the sky or the ten-foot whip antenna that stuck out of their back, they were a primary target of enemy fire. The antenna also was a pinpoint for mortar attack from afar. It was as if everywhere they went, they announced, "I'm right here." It was often said that in a firefight, the radiomen had a life expectancy of five seconds. While that might be an exaggeration, the reality wasn't much longer. The enemy lusted to destroy the ability of the recon unit to communicate.

The radiomen also were typically the last to board the choppers when the unit extracted from a mission, keeping communication alive until it was no longer necessary from the ground. In addition, the enemy understood that the radioman humped directly behind the man in charge, giving them a chance at taking out the two most important elements of the patrol at once.

When a firefight unfolded, members of the unit tried to keep a keen eye on the location of the radioman, for he was their only connection to ultimate safety. Get separated from the radioman and potentially stranded, and a Marine could be literally on his own, untethered from help, lost in the vast maze of the jungle, on a countdown to death.

Rifleman. The essential function of the rifleman was to be prepared for combat. Like the point man, he might double as the assistant patrol leader. While the overriding mission of reconnaissance units was to gather intelligence, the reality was that often, and more often than military command preferred or liked to think, recon units engaged the enemy. It wasn't something that could be avoided by choice. It was a jungle war, and each day was as unpredictable as the next. The rifleman, carrying his M16 and M79, as well as a cache of grenades and his Ka-Bar, had to be battle-ready each step of the way.

The Marines have a Rifle Creed. It goes like this:

1. *This is my rifle. There are many like it, but this one is mine.*
2. *My rifle is my best friend. It is my life. I must master it as I must master my life.*
3. *My rifle, without me, is useless. Without my rifle, I am useless. I must fire my rifle true. I must shoot straighter than my enemy who is trying to kill me. I must shoot him before he shoots me. I will . . .*

4. My rifle and myself know that what counts in this war is not the rounds we fire, the noise of our burst, nor the smoke we make. We know that it is the hits that count. We will hit...

5. My rifle is human, even as I, because it is my life. Thus, I will learn it as a brother. I will learn its weaknesses, its strength, its parts, its accessories, its sights and its barrel. I will ever guard it against the ravages of weather and damage as I will ever guard my legs, my arms, my eyes and my heart against damage. I will keep my rifle clean and ready. We will become part of each other. We will...

6. Before God, I swear this creed. My rifle and myself are the defenders of my country. We are the masters of our enemy. We are the saviors of my life.

7. So be it, until victory is America's and there is no enemy, but peace!!

Secondary Radioman. Because of the vital importance of the primary radioman and the high risk of death he faced, the recon unit included a secondary radioman on patrol. It was common for the secondary radioman to tuck his antenna under his shirt to conceal his role to the enemy.

The availability of a second mode of communication also improved the ability of the unit to communicate with base camp and pilots. The two radiomen used different codes. This was particularly helpful when the unit engaged the enemy, and the two radiomen got separated and had to hunker down at different places in the field.

Corpsman. Each recon team had an assigned doctor, a Navy corpsman, the Army equivalent of a medic. They were invaluable, and their medical responsibilities ran the gamut. At one end of the spectrum, they played faux military mom, making sure everyone took their malaria pills and had relatively clean water, reprimanding about poor hygiene, tending to jungle rot, providing tetanus shots and emulsions for head lice, and treating garden-variety illnesses that infected unit members. At the other end of the spectrum, they were first responders to treat trauma suffered from hostile or combat environments, galvanized to action by the unmistakable call alert, "Corpsman up!" In this capacity, the corpsman dealt with a wide range of wounds, from treating gunshot and shrapnel lacerations to applying tourniquets to body parts that once had limbs. They often had a front-row seat to the arrival of death.

The recon unit went to great pains to protect its corpsman. Like the radioman, the corpsman was on the priority kill list of the enemy, and in the absence of special protection, had a similarly short life expectancy during a firefight or ambush. The consequences of losing medical help were severe, increasing the risk of death and complications from wounds and giving the enemy an enormous battle advantage. Whenever practical, the patrol leader found ways to keep the corpsman out of harm's way. While corpsmen were known to engage in battles out of necessity, they were generally kept out of firefights to be available for medical needs. There was an understood quid quo pro: the unit protected the corpsman, and the corpsman took care of the unit.

Corpsmen were endowed with a rare form of implicit authority. Their medical training decreed that in combat, they could override a superior ranking soldier in any lifesaving situation, whether dealing with a fellow Marine or confronting a captured enemy. A patrol leader might not pay this heed. But if a conflict ripened, a corpsman might be forced to test the bounds of his medical oath and risk a court-martial by disobeying an order in the field (as will be seen later).

Tail-end Charlie. The last recon man along the trail, the tail-end Charlie was responsible for keeping an eye on the rear flank. Like the point man and patrol leader, he was responsible for reading the environment for signs of danger or other evidence of military significance but from the rear. And, like the rifleman, the tail-end Charlie had to be combat-ready.

The recon unit was the peak embodiment of esprit de corps. It's hard to imagine any team or group achieving the degree and power of trust, bond, and common purpose found in reconnaissance units. For sure, it likely had to do with what was at stake and the odds of survival and death we faced virtually each day. But whatever it was, those seven men became an uncommon, unified force that defied replication.

My Recon Team (me front row, far right)

⬤ 5 ⬤

THE UNSUNG RECON HEROES

It is amazing what you can accomplish if
you do not care who gets the credit.
—Harry S. Truman, former U.S. president
and colonel in the U.S. Army

When recon missions succeeded, when the results lined up well with military leadership's expectations, patrol teams got some credit and sometimes praise.

That, I suppose, was to be expected. We were, after all, the most visible. Our frontline roles made it easy to portray us on center stage. The stuff made good copy for the daily military newspaper *Stars and Stripes* and other media: the reconnaissance patrol team, deep within enemy-controlled territory, carrying out their charge valiantly, at great risk to their lives, humping jungle terrain, battling elements, and skillfully evading or engaging the enemy eyeball to eyeball.

But recon patrol teams didn't operate alone. On the contrary. The success of recon work and the safe return of patrol members depended on many other fellow Marines, the unsung heroes of reconnaissance operations. Those background players put their lives at risk to save ours. They, no less than we, answered the call of duty with selflessness and courage, often going about their business in the shadows, without seeking attention. They did the jobs they were asked to do, and they did them well.

But they rarely got the credit they richly deserved. It is important to give them due recognition.

THE PURPLE FOXES.

The Marine Medium Squadron 364 or HMM 364—better known as the Purple Foxes—was a helicopter squadron. During my time in-country, they deployed at Marble Mountain, a Marine aviation facility near Da Nang amid a cluster of five stunning marble and limestone hills. Like Camp Reasoner, the Marble Mountain aviation facility was wire-wrapped and guarded with sentry posts at entrances. Except for aviation storage hangars, it included the normal array of camp structures, including administrative buildings, officer quarters, and billeting for noncommissioned personnel, including flight crews. It was a functional location for aviation, high up on a ridge, but also within striking distance of enemy mortars and rockets, which sometimes disrupted life there and inflicted damage on exposed helicopters.

The Purple Foxes flew the Boeing CH-46 Sea Knight helicopter, one of the prime U.S. Marine troop transport aerial machines in Vietnam. When on recon missions, the CH-46 crew normally included the pilot (helicopter aircraft commander or HAC), a co-pilot, a crew chief, and two machine gunners, all taking their positions at the front of the chopper.

The gunners used .50 caliber machine guns weighing about forty pounds. They were more than five feet long and temporarily attached to the chopper floor. The .50 caliber guns were loaded with one hundred rounds, which the crew could replenish with the ten additional boxes of one hundred rounds stored for each gun. They were well stacked.

In situations with heightened concerns, the CH-46 crew added a third gunner equipped with an M60 machine gun. Weighing almost twenty-five pounds, the M60 was a gas-operated, air-cooled, belt-fed automatic machine gun that in the field normally took two or three men to operate. In a CH-46, the gunner handled those responsibilities alone, bracing the M60 in his lap.

In addition, the HAC, copilot, and crew chief carried a sidearm, either a .45 or .38 pistol, in addition to the M16 that everyone, including the patrol team, brought as a matter of course.

The CH-46 pilots and crews participated in several notable military operations during the Vietnam War, flying over 70,000 hours in combat and combat support missions. It is no surprise that the powers that be awarded the HHM-364 the Presidential Unit Citation for meritorious conduct in the performance of duty. They were fearless and excelled in what they did.

The commander of the Purple Foxes liked to say, "Sometimes you just have to give a shit."

The Purple Foxes, with their CH-46s, were our essential recon transportation. They were responsible for taking us safely from Camp Reasoner to the site of our insertion into the jungle and returning days later to the designated extraction site to retrieve and return us to base camp.

Each early morning of a mission, as we started our groggy-headed stroll toward the takeoff location before the sun had peeked over the horizon, the CH-46 crew would be waiting for us. They had received their briefing, did their preflight check, loaded their weaponry and ammo, had their second breakfast (courtesy of Camp Reasoner), and rechecked their systems. Each time, without exception, they'd be laser focused and ready to go.

We didn't exchange words with the crew. They focused on their roles. We focused on ours. We boarded from the back while the crew got situated in the front. We sat in silence among ourselves, left to whatever thoughts we had about what we were about to do. The crew and the patrol team worked together alone.

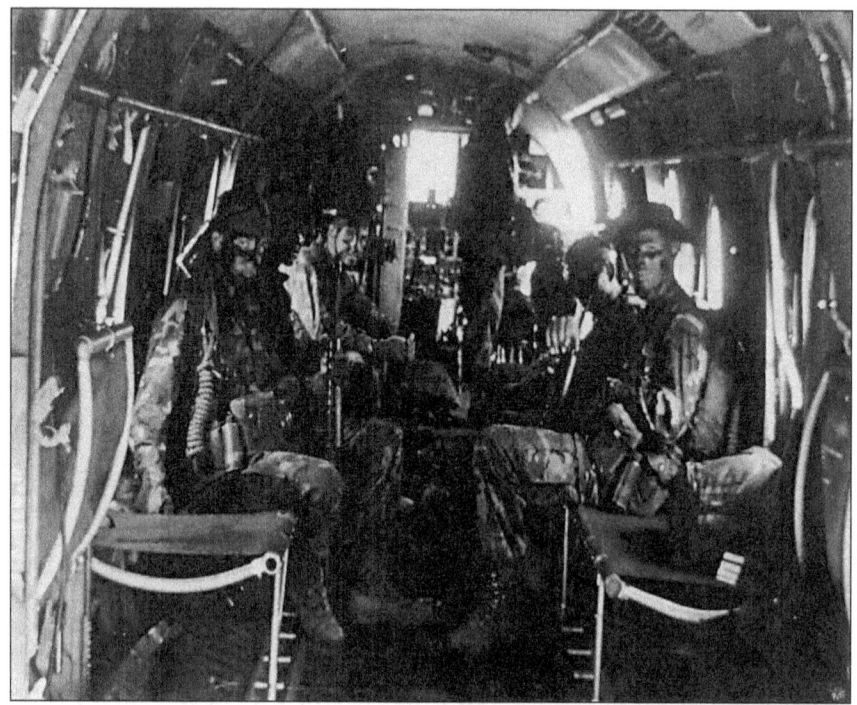

Enroute to an Insertion

On typical patrols, two CH-46s handled the chores. The first, the lead chopper, transported the patrol team and whatever we took with us. The second chopper, the chase chopper, followed behind to provide protection, making sure the recon team got inserted safely.

Once airborne, the lead aircraft might get a supplemental report from scout planes picking up new information to help with the flight and insertion. Otherwise, we flew among the clouds waiting to land at our designated insertion spot with the initial game plan in hand.

Most insertions went easily. Sometimes, however, the insertion locale was too hot, forcing a search for a different spot. Other times, the CH-46 feigned an insertion to throw off the enemy.

And, other times still, because of the difficult terrain or obstructive tree lines, the planned insertion landing zone was inaccessible, requiring we insert by rappelling down a rope unfurled from the chopper. In those detour circumstances, you never knew how it might play out, other than the Purple Fox crew doing their level best to deposit us as safely as possible.

Retrieving us a few days later, after we had completed our missions, wasn't as seamless and straightforward as picking us up at the start. We took off in our backyard, from our home base. We got extracted from the backyard of the enemy. In the back of our minds, extraction was always an uncertainty. The back end didn't always go according to plan. It could get downright hairy, as will be seen later.

The CH-46 crews who transported us had courage and bravery to spare. They were noble and loyal, and consistently took risks to support our missions beyond what anyone could reasonably expect. The Purple Foxes were all in.

One example concerns Dennis Welsch, whom I grew up with in Marin County and who served in Vietnam at the same time I did, mostly as a gunner with the Purple Foxes. Amazingly, neither of us were aware the other was in-country, even though it is likely that Dennis handled an insertion or two for my recon unit. This was unbeknownst to either of us, owing to camouflage and that the recon unit sat at the back of the choppers while the gunners were up front, plus the somber introspective mentality we brought to the ride en route to our missions. Dennis was a badass, and as a Marine, no doubt, was selfless and courageous, which military leadership was quick to acknowledge.

Shortly after Dennis returned to The World, President Lyndon Johnson awarded him the Air Medal (the aerial equivalent of the Bronze Star), which President Franklin Roosevelt inaugurated in 1942 to recognize heroic achievement in aerial flight during combat operations.

During the night of March 28, 1970, Dennis was a gunner on one of two CH-46s that command officers sent to conduct an emergency extraction of a seven-man reconnaissance unit that had become compromised after contact with the enemy and was in severe danger. By the time CH-46s arrived, the recon unit was hunkered down beyond a defensive perimeter and taking enemy fire from all sides. They were grossly outnumbered, and without a chopper extraction, no question, each would be killed or captured. They had no other exit but the sky.

The citation states, among other things:

> Corporal Welsch resolutely manned his weapon and boldly delivered a steady stream of accurate and highly effective machine gun fire which suppressed the hostile fire sufficiently to enable his helicopter to remain in its precarious position until all of the Marines had attached themselves to the [extraction] ladder. He continued to maintain his devastating fire while his aircraft lifted out of the dangers area.... Corporal Welsh's courage, superior professionalism, and unwavering devotion to duty in the face of great personal danger were instrumental in accomplishing the hazardous mission and in keeping with the highest traditions of the Marine Corps and the United States Naval Service.

Recon Make VC Lead Rough Life

DANANG — Imagine, if you will, returning home from the day long work of laying booby traps, hiding from the enemy in the air and on the ground and finishing other innumerable tasks assigned you as a VC guerrilla or NVA soldier.

Home is a shelter or bunker set deep in a ravine, cleverly concealed to offer protection from the enemy forces.

Upon arrival home you find papers strewn about — Chieu Hoi "Open Arms" leaflets, calling on you to rally to the side of the government of the Republic of Vietnam.

You've seen these Chieu Hoi leaflets dropped from the air into open arms, but never in an area you considered your own private bastion.

During an unwatched moment, you take out the puzzling leaflet, study it and wonder how it got to where you found it. Reading the message gives no clue to solve the mystery.

You turn the leaflet over, gazing at the emblem and the message to you; it's from the "eyes of the 1st Marine Division" — 1st Reconnaissance Bn. Then you realize that these leaflets weren't dropped from the air. Someone was here, knows where you are, and maybe, is watching you now.

Through the twilight, that silent thought is with you, and as you prepare to sleep that night you look about wondering if instead of a message under your rice bowl tomorrow you will find a patrol of these "swift, silent and deadly" Marines waiting on your doorstep.

. . . With The Greatest Of Ease

Team members from the Marine 1st Reconnaissance Battalion sail through the air more than 1,500 feet above Thu Bon River on their way to An Hoa Combat Base. The team was operating in an area 28 miles south-southwest of Da Nang when they called for an emergency extraction after being surrounded by NVA soldiers.   (USMC PHOTO By: Capt. J. P. Novak)

Emergency extractions were far too common

THE OV-10 AND BELL AH-1.

The Marines used two other aircraft to assist in our missions: the OV-10 and the Bell AH-1. The OV-10, called the Bronco, filled a wide range of roles, including forward air controller, radio relay station, artillery spotter, helicopter escort, visual reconnaissance, convoy escort, and not the least, to launch an attack. Among other weaponry, it was armed with a Gatling gun and seven-shot rocket pods with white phosphorus marker rounds and high-explosive rockets.

Since the CH-46s and the Purple Foxes were our main ride to and from the mission, the Broncos got called in whenever we were in trouble, like when we needed extra help fending off an attack or artillery cover to gain safety en route to an extraction site.

The Bell AH-1, or Cobra, was a single-engine attack helicopter and a member of the renowned Huey family of aviation machines. The AH-1 is often referred to as the Huey Cobra or Snake.

Originally designed for the Army, the Cobra became an attack chopper for the Marines in Vietnam. For our purposes in reconnaissance, the Cobra often functioned like the Bronco, playing the role of lifesaver, coming to aid in situations to provide fire support for us on the ground. The Cobra Gatling guns, with outputs of about 2,000 rounds, could be disruptive, spraying the jungle top to bottom, forcing the enemy to retreat or take severe casualties. The Cobras usually had a crew of two: pilot and copilot/gunner.

The Broncos and Cobras were badasses in the jungle. When they arrived on a scene, they made their presence known. They could turn the tables around quickly and decisively, becoming the difference in whether a patrol team survived or not.

When these various helicopter crews—the CH-46s, Broncos, and Cobras—got their orders to fly, they couldn't care less whether they were headed into inhospitable territory. They got the nod and off they went. Sometimes they took fire going in, and sometimes they took fire going out and sometimes at both ends. When we'd disembark at Camp Reasoner, we sometimes noticed how much the big bird exterior resembled Swiss cheese from the countless rounds they took during their missions. One pilot told us, "You're not fearful because you're going to get hurt. You're fearful because you're going to hurt somebody else if you don't do your job right."

God bless them.

Each member of the helicopter crews who handled our transportation and bailed us out of major jams deserves respect and recognition. In each their own way, they helped me stay alive and return home. I can never repay them. As one Purple Fox gunner put it, his greatest contribution as a Marine in Vietnam was "saving lives."

MILITARY INTELLIGENCE

I need to mention one other group of the extended patrol team, the personnel who did their jobs behind closed doors: military intelligence officers who crafted our missions and gave us our orders.

In honesty, I thought that sometimes they sent us on virtual suicide missions, military gambits that posed unnecessary risks, playing us as pawns in a back room military game that fed their hunger for power, without corresponding military value. I feared what I might do in those days if I ever came face-to-face with anyone responsible for sending us out on insane missions, putting my life and those of my comrades at severe risk. We took to calling them REMFs, otherwise known as rear echelon motherfuckers, not a term of military endearment.

Of course, I didn't participate in the situational and strategy sessions. I never knew the specifics of what went down in those brainstorming gatherings. I didn't know the underlying thinking or various considerations. The contents were classified. And, I am sure, some of what was decided got handed down from up the chain of command. But as time passed, as the war faded to a nagging blur in the rearview window of my soul, I came to appreciate the value of our recon missions and how the intelligence we gathered saved lives and prevented further destruction. I know for some, especially nonmilitary, that perspective might be a difficult pill to swallow, since the war for them represents at best a zero-sum game and at worst an unjustified carnage and unwarranted intervention into the civil affairs of a small nation. I respect that view. But taking the war as a reality, and accepting the cards dealt us Marines, but for reconnaissance operations, things would likely have been considerably worse.

I bow to the various military personnel who worked with us to help execute the orders we received as reconnaissance Marines. Each contributed as part of a well-coordinated, concerted effort. Each deserves credit and praise.

Warming Up for the Next Aerial Mission

— 6 —

A DIFFERENT KIND OF SAVIOR

> We cannot pass our guardian angel's bounds,
> resigned or sullen; he will hear our sighs.
> — Saint Augustine

R ecognizing unsung heroes in this Vietnam War narrative would not be complete without specially honoring and expounding on the work of the extraordinary men who navigated the Broncos.

Bronco design specifications, in theory at least, gave pilots implied permission to fly as high as 26,000 feet and, as constructed, allowed operation at the tops of the triple-canopy jungle at 300 feet in favorable conditions. But that was theory.

In jungle warfare, in reality, the versatile Bronco and its fearless Marine crews commonly flew at 1,500 feet or lower to do their jobs, dangerously close to where enemy ground fire could reach them.

The Bronco normally housed two men: the pilot and an aerial observer (AO). Both were typically officers with flight and combat training. Bronco pilots and AOs, like other Marine aircraft personnel, endured boot camp and infantry training with the rest of us, ensuring they had an early ingrained infantry mind-set. So, from day one, those destined to navigate big Bronco birds in the jungle became immersed in on-the-ground training and integrated with us. They knew, as a result, how to relate to and communicate with troops on the ground.

Both men typically flew alone together, the AO behind the pilot in the cockpit. The two were, figuratively and literally, joined at the hip. They functioned with a command ejection system. If one pulled, the other automatically followed five seconds later.

Bronco crews often flew with the CH-46 helicopters at night to maintain their requisite hours, spending much time in the wee hours making rough landings. No rest for the weary.

As noted, the Bronco came equipped with a 20 mm cannon in the front, underneath the seat of the AO; four M60 machine guns on the wings, and two rocket pods that could launch both high explosives and white phosphorus for marking grounds. The pilot was responsible for handling all weaponry, while the AO directed the action, "putting smoke" where it would do the most help. If, for example, a recon patrol was in trouble on one side of a river, getting pummeled by the enemy on the other side, the AO was charged with making sure the pilot, or other artillery called in, put smoke on the enemy side, especially jets and other aircraft a distance away that lacked the same ability to pinpoint desired targets.

Bronco crews were fearless and tireless. Their main job was to fly, gather intelligence, observe recon areas, stay connected with recon teams, and if and when the teams got in trouble, bring fury to the situation. While Bronco crews, like recon patrol units, normally had a mission before hitting the skies, sometimes they got called in to an emergency—TIC (troops in contact)—while doing general reconnaissance. In TIC situations, whatever else they were doing became secondary. Broncos were a little like free agents, roaming the jungle, checking things, and waiting for the military version of a 911 call to help a recon team in the shit, either employing direct engagement, putting down suppressive fire from above, or calling in air action. In all cases, they functioned as the controller of everybody coming to help. Because boots on the ground were often on the move or fiercely embattled, they struggled to communicate with other incoming help like the Cobras or the jets with heavier firepower. The Bronco handled the frontline communication.

Emergencies—the unpredictability of never-ending jungle warfare—were commonplace in Vietnam, so much so that Bronco crews often went to bed at night wearing necklaces bearing a plastic card with grid coordinates for the recon teams humping jungle in the darkness. When called upon in the dead of night, the pilot revved up the engines and got ready to soar, while the AO plotted precisely how and where they were headed and what they'd likely face on arrival. There was always a crew on the "hot pad" ready to go.

They flew each time knowing they faced daunting odds of survival. Rare was the Bronco crew who ditched their bird in a crisis, catapulted out, and survived. They were all-in for their jobs, and their jobs were to save the rest of us. For their part, successful mission or not, their survival depended on a safe return by air. Hope may have sprung eternal for others, but for the Bronco crews, the prospects of a reckoning consistently hovered nearby.

That is because their intervention often caused the enemy to salivate. Now, rather than care so much about the boots on the ground, the enemy might refocus their efforts on the bigger prize, taking out an aircraft. It was common for Broncos and other aircraft within ground-striking distance to take serious fire, often with horrendous results. They were a bigger fish. The enemy wanted a Cobra, Sea Knight, or Bronco. They wanted bragging rights. And they didn't need more than standard issue, the AK-47, which, if close enough, could hit fuel tanks and hydraulics, and then it might be all over. In that way, it was like taking out a corpsman or radioman, robbing the unit of their lifeline.

As extra insurance, Bronco crew members carried inside their lower right pockets a personal "blood sheet," a silk scarf emblazoned with an American flag that bore the words in five local dialects: "You get my ass somewhere safe, you're going to make a lot of money." If an aircraft went down, that thin piece of cloth served as a lottery ticket promising a handsome bounty for local villagers who helped return the downed crew—assuming the enemy didn't capture them first.

On average, a Bronco crew handled three missions a day. What were the odds of one over time becoming fatal?

The enemy wasn't their only concern. Precision weighed heavily. Whenever called upon to intervene in the mission of others, they had an abiding fear they might call in an air strike to assist recon units in distress and deliver instead friendly fire on their comrades or civilians in the midst. The danger thus was not only identifying targets clearly but being acutely aware of the location of friendly forces, no easy task in the vision-limiting jungle with the ever-present camouflage, the mind-boggling confusion in the heat of battle, occasional technical difficulties with radios, and lightning-speed changes in circumstances.

They suffered terrifying moments when they unleashed cover or called in an airstrike and then radioed for assurance that all was okay only to hear nothing in return, keeping them anxious about the results of their intervention. Was everyone okay? Was the enemy still coming? Did we have friendly fire casualties? Was more help needed? Sometimes all was good. The lapse in communication was a natural progression of war in the jungle. Sometimes it would be bad. In both cases, the seemingly forever interlude of not knowing haunted them.

Yet, with uncommon devotion, they hugged tightly to the mission and their charge. They developed a keen sense of immortality, not in the sense of personal invulnerability, but of the powerful internal feeling they could always save, always be there to rescue us with little or no fear for themselves. They were all about others, true heroes.

Much of their success and effectiveness depended on how well the AO managed communications. The AO had to be radio proficient, as communication with ground forces and headquarters was essential to doing their job effectively and with swift dispatch. The communication stream started immediately on lift-off from the pad, after getting briefed on the mission. The first order of business once in the air was getting an acute bead on the human trail below. As they did, the communication and navigation challenges steadily piled up, and they endured a variety of impediments, including limited jungle visibility, fog, rain, and whatever else the jungle wanted to throw their way.

The AO manned six different radio channels, often unleashing a flood of data that filtered through his head. He pushed this and that button to connect, moving back and forth, not losing sight of the several secret codes to facilitate rapid-fire communication in the heat of the moment, adjusting volumes to decipher essential information or favor a source that seemed more important than the others. He did all this while providing information to the pilot to assist with aerial navigation.

To help coordinate a location, they'd often "lay in a smoke," directing the unit on the ground to use a white phosphorus grenade to create a billowy phosphorus cloud to function as a landmark to allow the Bronco to pinpoint the location. The rub was that the crafty and resourceful enemy might lay their own smoke to confuse and entice aircraft to fire at the wrong location, increasing chances of friendly fire casualties. Coordinating different colors minimized that risk, but friendly fire casualties constantly loomed as a major problem in such circumstances. Alternatively, they'd flash mirrors instead, which normally the enemy couldn't detect, a flicker of light eking out of the chaos to identify the location.

It could get so hectic, loud, and furious that the pilot and AO would communicate with each other by hand signals, looking at each other via mirrors in the cabin. To complicate matters, the lower they flew, the greater the gravitational force against their bodies, making concentration a major challenge. Worse still, helmets in relentless jungle heat became like a big sponge, and the flood of compressed sweat ran all over their faces and into their eyes. They'd wear scarves in anticipation, and when they could, would free one hand to wipe the burning salt from their eyes so they could see well enough to do their job—for the pilot perhaps to clear a mountain and the AO to navigate the path and continue with radio contact.

It would often be an extraordinary demonstration of managing many balls in the air, an artistic virtuoso performance that would make any top-shelf magician proud. They knew that a single miscue, a missed message, or frequency error could cost lives, including their own.

The Bronco was not the final answer. They were there to provide cover and support to hold a situation while greater firepower could be unleashed: more air support, more artillery and heavy weaponry, and eventually the arrival of another bird to extract the boots on the ground. They were not there to function as Wild West gunfighters, but rather to function as stopgaps to keep embattled comrades safe and the enemy at bay before more muscle like fire support assets or an extraction crew arrived. Because of their superior vantage points, they might also direct a recon unit to a safer location to gain time for a CH-46 extraction.

Broncos were, for most intents and purposes, first responders, keeping things under control temporarily while other help made its way to the scene. They were not designed to handle a major shoot-up. Once they performed their function, they'd be gone, returning to their original mission or going on to the next crisis.

The importance of the impromptu intervention of the Bronco and its crew whenever the shit hit the fan cannot be stressed enough. They were like anonymous guardian angels. They'd appear, do their thing, save lives, and disappear into the sky, most likely never seen again by those who benefited from their timely courage and heroism. A well-deserved deep bow to them, with specific application as will be seen later.

7

THE JUNGLE

> Into the forest I go, to lose my mind and find my soul.
> — John Muir

Before we got on that plane to Southeast Asia, they warned us. They told us about the sweltering and suffocating heat of the Vietnam jungle, soon to become our residence for thirteen grueling months—if, of course, we were so lucky. We were trained to survive what we were assured was nothing like we'd ever experienced or could possibly imagine.

Little did we know.

I got my first good look at the Vietnam jungle and its renowned triple canopy early one groggy morning when a thick embankment of fog burnt off, sending puffs of milky mist skyward. It was like a curtain rising to reveal a brilliant set design on a performance stage.

As an avid outdoors person, I basked in the wonders of the natural landscape. I loved being outside and spent considerable time exploring the many hiking and running trails in my beloved home community of Marin County, California. It was in that setting where I often quieted my mind and connected with myself. I reveled in the beauty of the physical world.

The Vietnam jungle, however, was something else to behold. Above the understory layer was the primary layer with growth of sixty to ninety feet, and then further up an emergent layer with growth as high as three hundred feet, with trunks fifteen feet around and mushroom-cap crowns. While I felt the power of its mystique from a distance, putting our small and insignificant existence in perspective, anxiety brewed in my stomach about what it might have in store.

The Vietnam rainforest, we would learn, was more than a vision of sheer beauty. It was an ecological treasure trove, home to millions of species of plants and exotic flowers and a bountiful source of food and medicine. It provided life and shelter to dozens of primates, including gibbons and snub-nosed monkeys, as well as tigers, elephants, bears, leopards, deer, wild boars, cobras, other snakes, the dreaded bamboo vipers, pythons, scorpions, a regiment of mosquitos, large and small nasty leeches, various spiders, and not the least, the legendary and irascible Rock Apes.

The Vietnam jungle was a temple where interdependent organisms gathered and connected in the natural order of things.

But such romantic reflections had limited relevance to the jungle we were to experience and come to know. You will never find *that* jungle, the jungle of war, in a travel brochure or holiday advertisement. Whatever our naïveté and soon-to-be lost innocence, we knew we hadn't come a third of the way across the globe to commune with nature and collect vacation photos to display back home. We were there to fight a war, engage in battle without choice, and, yes, kill. There would be no ritual path to the altars of the mythical war gods. Ours was a destructive path and our presence the antithesis of everything natural and spiritual in that natural wonder.

The jungle didn't make it any easier, to understate the reality of things. By its very nature, it kept you uncomfortable. It always seemed to have eyes on us, know our every step, hear our every breath, take note of our fear, hidden or not. Sometimes it felt like the trees and jungle brush talked about us in code, assessing us, thinking about what to do with us. It was a pulsating, living organism that on a whim could absorb us into its soul, like the biblical whale did Jonah.

And where is the enemy?

For sure, there would be moments during military exercise downtime when the surroundings quieted enough for us to appreciate their magnificence. But those moments evaporated quickly, on a natural whim.

The stark truth was that in the deep pockets of our military calling, the jungle was a take-no-prisoners, merciless, and confounding place we'd long to forget and never could, no matter how hard we'd try or how much prayer we offered our deities of choice.

For our part, we battled the darn thing and tried to overcome it. We swore at it. We chopped and hacked away at its thick foliage, and sometimes with our vast military might, destroyed parts of it. We disturbed and violated its tranquility.

We knew where we stood. We were intruders and plunderers.

Where is the enemy?

We often had a warm-up before engaging the jungle's tangled web. We first had to survive the vicious elephant grass as we made our way to the jungle. Growing as high as seven feet and dominating hundreds of meters of jungle terrain, elephant grass collected in bunches under trees and alongside riverbanks. Its nastiest feature was its razor-sharp edges, which sliced and diced our bodies, drawing blood, slicing jungle utilities, and ripping the gloves we sometimes wore to minimize damage to our hands from the brush. Elephant grass was ruthless.

Once at the jungle entrance, under the lightless shroud of the tree canopies, we had the distinction of being greeted by the jungle's gatekeepers: a steady stream of bloodsucking, slime-coated jungle leeches. Grotesque members of the worm family in seemingly inexhaustible supply, leeches rained down on us from gargantuan leaves above, like the B-52s our Air Force dropped on Vietnam and neighboring nations. They focused with laser precision on their landing zones of choice, a grimy neck, a camouflage-darkened face, an exposed hand or wrist, or an inviting, exposed, muscled back. If they missed their targets from on high, they hugged the jungle floor, waiting to attach to a boot in search of lower leg flesh. If you tried to foil them by filling your boots with pant legs, they'd find a rip or tear, channeling a sordid beeline to private parts.

Leeches had an uncanny ability for finding skin after nosediving from above or, in the case of their larger, water-based cousins, after lying in wait in the mud-filled swollen streams and rivers where we carried weapons over our heads and sixty-pound packs on our backs. They were relentless, resourceful, and unforgiving, and we were easy pickings.

Once they found their targets, the ghastly creatures began their blood feast, inserting their proboscis, a slender sucking organ, into the flesh like a hypodermic needle, drawing an amount of blood grossly out of proportion to their own weight, as much as five times greater. Often, they'd get so bloated they'd burst, like a water balloon pricked with a needle, splattering your own blood all over you. It seemed almost comical—almost.

Removing leeches wasn't always easy. Most of the time, you could feel and find them. But dealing with them meant breaking the flow of movement on the trail, and that didn't fit well with the military mission. We had to keep humping the jungle. Precision mattered. The leeches weren't a life threat. They only craved their Dracula moment. So, unless we could swat them off quickly, we suffered them until a pause allowed patrol buddies to burn them off with a cigarette or with one of our most valuable weapons of war, insect repellant we called "jungle juice," which we hauled in generous quantities.

Using jungle juice to rid our bodies of leeches, however, came with a price. No matter how careful we were, it was next to impossible to stop the jungle juice from seeping into an array of sores, bites, abrasions, and blisters we collected on our hands and arms from the ordeal of breaking brush. When that happened, we suffered a vicious burning sensation that lasted hours.

The leeches were the jungle's wicked price of admission, its way of saying, "You're not welcome here, but if you insist on entering..."

So, right off, we got a clear message. We didn't belong, and we'd pay for our presence each day multiple times and in multiple ways. Nothing would come easy. We had to find ways to cope, to recalibrate tolerance levels. We had to find comfort where comfort wasn't natural. We had to reform ourselves and become someone we'd never known before.

Where is the enemy?

We weren't always left to our own devices. Native jungle creatures left clues for us, much like enemy activity did. The presence and absence of certain species, especially monkeys, held military significance. Our enemy dined on monkeys, evidently their out-in-the-boonies primitive meal of choice. If we didn't smell or hear monkeys in the area, the odds of lurking danger increased, as the presence of the monkey-eating enemy likely had driven the resident primates to a sanctuary. Monkeys knew who liked to eat them. Conversely, if we heard, smelled, or saw monkeys, while we were never safe, ever, chances were that we weren't about to engage the enemy any time soon.

Similarly, birds tended to be sources of military information. Like monkeys and the Rock Apes, birds traveled in large groups most of the time. If someone flushed the group, for example, like an NVA unit killed a bird, that would drive them out. You could have birds coming toward you, making a quick exodus. The same might apply to deer, often the size of dogs, barking in the night, in some form of panic or stress. It meant one of two things: either a forest fire or an NVA unit on a sweep looking for food. The NVA had horrible noise discipline. If you heard birds or saw deer doing their business calmly, you could fairly assume no one else was nearby. If they seemed agitated or were making a quick getaway, the enemy was likely near.

Elephants were helpful in their own way, although we almost never saw them. They were fast and supple and didn't stick around long and managed to avoid visual detection. But we heard and smelled them, and they, of course, left evidence of their existence in the form of ample piles of dung. Moving as a caravan, they'd often blaze a wide berth of trail that gave us additional terrain to traverse. Often, their personalized trails were fresh and tended to be safe, at least relatively safe, given where we were.

Was that Charlie?

Walking is where the jungle turned the most normal of things on its head. The jungle floor, lying below three canopies of growth, was a constantly murky surface that enjoyed sparse sunlight. Because the sun had great difficulty reaching the floor through the triple canopy, to survive, plants stretched mightily in search of sunlight, and as a result grew enormous leaves and bamboo taller than any Marine stood. The result was a formidable barricade so impenetrable you could fall forward and be held upright. It was as if the jungle wrapped its arms around our lower torsos and held tight.

We trudged through that morass as if slogging through a deep snowbank. As quietly as possible, we unwound the tangled vines and used our Ka-Bars to cut and slice through the undergrowth. We hacked whatever clogged our passage. Unlike other patrol units, we didn't have the luxury of machetes to chomp our way through the solid brush. Machetes were heavy and would have added substantially to our carry. They also are noisemakers, increasing the risk of pinging eager enemy ears. We had to make do with Ka-Bars, our standard-issue combat knife, a foot long with a seven-inch blade, weighing about half a pound, a child's instrument compared with what the legendary Jim Bowie was renowned to have used. Unlike a machete, the Ka-Bar was ill-equipped to shred the thick bamboo and grass, so we hacked away to move the jungle blockade aside enough to allow movement. It's no exaggeration to say we often spent more time chopping and cutting than walking. It was exhausting and molasses slow.

To make matters worse, we had to face the infamous "wait-a-minute vines," tenacious creepers with fishhook endings that would latch on to our utilities or a weapon and yank us off pace, sometimes dropping us to the moist jungle floor or dislodging a weapon from our grip. Wait-a-minute vines disrupted movement of the unit, putting us at greater risk.

No matter how valiant our efforts battling the forbidding brush, we couldn't avoid becoming draped in dampness. Jungle moisture from foliage, as well as the moist mud and muck on the ground below, soaked through our utilities. Some days we spent considerable time on our rears, slipping and sliding down hills and riverbeds. Add the rains, the unrelenting monsoons, the uncommon heat and humidity, and staying dry became the stuff of dreams. When the winds hit, racing through the triple canopy with extraordinary velocity, the body shuddered head to toe and teeth rattled.

Where is the enemy?

The pervasive dampness brought its own set of gifts, including dreaded jungle rot, an infection that oozed pus from our lower extremities and that we'd wipe on our utilities. The degradation plunged to a low point when old and new rot pus mixed with a concoction of leech blood, monsoon-dampened mud, grease from shitty K-rations, and whatever slimy crap we'd absorbed. Beyond disgusting.

Then there was immersion foot. The constant assault on the membranes of the feet and continuous pounding in soaked boots numbed our lower appendages and produced blisters and sores, and, in the worst case, gangrene. Immersion foot was a slowly developing affliction that snuck up until one day, after removing your boots to ease the pain, the grotesque damage was undeniable. If you ignored your foot condition long enough, foot rot and decaying blood from leeches would congeal and adhere in clumps to your feet.

We were at war with the jungle as well as with our designated enemy. We tried to manage both, perhaps tame them a little, secure some advantage, but we could never be David to their Goliath. We knew who had the power in this game. We had to find a way to survive on their terms.

* * *

While we battled against the leech assault and overcame breaking brush—and, oh yes, fended off the constant drone attacks of flies and malaria-infested mosquitoes—our bodies still faced monstrous, unrelenting heat. Well before the noon hour, the jungle became a literal pressure cooker as the thick tropical heat became entrapped inside the triple canopy. When combined with the other physical conditions, heat and humidity became a constant beatdown, stealing our energy each second. It made breathing difficult at first, which could become labored and then sparse and scary, requiring frequent stoppages, certainly more than military brass in the rear had wanted or planned. It could get to where rain was a godsend, to cool and soothe. You longed for the rare cool breeze, an indescribable rush you'd want to freeze forever but could enjoy only for a precious few seconds. It wasn't just the feeling of chill on your face that you craved, but how the breeze represented hope, hope that the world you left behind still existed and might welcome your return.

The unforgiving jungle made the pace of movement insufferable, forcing us to measure progress in tiny, painfully slow increments of one step forward at a time. It could take literally hours to go a few hundred yards, bringing everyone to sheer exhaustion. Those moments of utter depletion behind enemy lines is when you wondered how much you had left in the tank, or if your time had come, or whether you should even care.

That is when the jungle had you captive and when it became eerily seductive.

The jungle teased with an alternative, a better deal, and dared you to accept it, like the serpent did Adam and Eve. "There are other trails," it whispered in your ear, "well-worn drier surfaces outside the direct reach of the jungle terrain, where you can walk at a near normal pace, make up for lost time, and arrive at your destination with time to spare for a well-needed rest." Those trails afforded better visibility than the dark place you were in, where it was difficult at best to spot anything until it was upon you, where so many things can be hidden from view, like weapons and supply routes—and worst of all unseen snipers.

But it was always a Faustian bargain. A well-used open trail meant enemy forces were recent visitors who might not be far away—and may be dangerously close. The chances of engaging them, and not necessarily on your terms, were significantly heightened. Worse, the alternative trails almost assuredly were pregnant with booby traps. The enemy concealed them with a lattice of twigs, leaves, brush, or other overgrowth to blend with the natural landscape. If stepped on, the camouflage cover gave way, and the unsuspecting victim, under the gravitational force of his own weight, plummeted to the bottom of the pit where the bamboo stakes awaited to tear into flesh and shred muscle and tendon. The sharp stakes were often bathed with feces and urine to bring on serious infection. As noted, a punji pit incident brought chaos and medical attention, distracting and depleting the ranks to give advantage to any planned enemy ambush.

So, if taking the oft-traveled trail drastically increased the odds of mayhem or death, why bother?

You bothered because you were consumed with exhaustion and frustration. You bothered because you were mentally weakened and close to emotional collapse. You bothered because you had tired of the jungle and its brutal insensitivity and indifference. Having pushed you to the limits, like a fighter pounds an opponent to the ropes, the jungle was now seducing, taunting, and humiliating you, promising you a better several hours if you took the deal. Diverging from the military script and increasing the risks suddenly seemed a temptation worth indulging in. Sometimes we indulged.

Electing to tread the more dangerous path sensitized us even more to sounds, increasing tension. We had to be pin-drop quiet. We moved without conversation, using hand signals to communicate and to minimize the risk of giving away positions. Walking like a whisper, we tried to avoid breaking a branch or so much as disturbing foliage, normally harmless disturbances but which in the jungle of war could announce our presence amid the thick, stifling air around us. We had to master the art of stealth.

Every sound that wasn't yours stilled the heart. Was the clang in the distance a cow bell or the sound of enemy equipment bouncing about? Were the whistling sounds from the shudder of rustling leaves or enemy bodies moving through brush? Did that twig snap under the paw of an animal or the booted foot of an NVA soldier on patrol?

Then there were moments, frozen in time, when the point man crouched suddenly, halting the snake of men behind him, relocating everyone's hearts to their throats to await his next move. He combed the landscape, looking, hearing, smelling, and feeling, trying to find what's not visible, what may be waiting to kill. He couldn't afford to be wrong—for the sake of all.

You strained to hear more. You became a little jumpy. There was a palpable anxiety it might be *that* moment, when you'd cross the Jordan, even though you likely wouldn't hear whatever it was that killed you. Maybe that was a good thing. No plan was perfect. You were always playing the odds, except either way, or every way, you were screwed.

Eventually, seeming much longer than it was, the day oozed into night. One moment it was light, the next pitch-black, like the flip of a light switch, eliminating virtually all visibility.

Nighttime was a mixed blessing. The days humping the terrain made night a welcome interlude, a chance for respite and some sleep. But nighttime jungle sounds magnified. Jungle stillness could cover everyone in a blanket of apprehension and sometimes fear. The interplay of the wind and tree branches or the barely perceptible rustling of a lizard or snake on the ground could trigger a red alert. Some nights the collection of weird noises and sounds coming from the darkness kept you awake worrying. Is that the enemy out there? Are they close or approaching? Do they know we are here? Should I grab my weapon? Or is the jungle tormenting me, keeping me off-balance and under its spell?

You instinctively grouped the sounds into two categories: safe or unsafe. Either way, they had your attention. Either way, it deepened your accumulated anxiety.

If the nighttime sounds didn't unnerve you, the ants might. Jungle ants were everywhere, vicious red devils, the infamous weaver ants. Once we settled in to an NDF (nighttime defensive position), those creepy crawlers often overran us, feasting on us no less ravenously than did leeches. They bit, and bit hard, injecting formic acid into the skin to stimulate intense localized pain. Like leeches, the red ants had a fondness for private parts. But unlike leeches, they seemed immune to jungle juice. Because a high risk of danger inhibited relocation, we had to succumb, letting the ants have their way with us.

The morning brought a time-honored ritual. Whether you slept well or not, a distinct possibility existed that leeches had found you during the night and made their way into you, literally. We each had an assigned buddy, affectionately called your "asshole buddy." We'd pair up in the morning, drop our drawers, and spread our butt cheeks so our asshole buddy could examine our asses for leeches. Any that were found met the fate of iodine or salt. There was no exchange of words, no expression of gratitude, no tribal chant. It was just done before we got to enjoy breakfast, our one meal of the day.

The dawn of each day tested us anew. Would we succumb to the spirits of war or reclaim ourselves? Would we surrender and die or inch ever closer to home?

Deep down we knew our chances of survival required enduring the heat, cold, mud, single-minded leeches and other insects, the impenetrable brush, piercing winds, the wet, malaria, jungle rot, immersion foot, scrapes, blisters and cuts, headaches, dehydration, shitty food, exhaustion, suffering, and monsoons. We had to let it bring us to the brink, test us beyond anything we had prepared for, push us to where all we had left were fumes from diminishing brain waves. We had to find a way to keep moving forward, fulfill military mandates, acutely aware that the future held the promise of more disgust, pain, and suffering. We persevered and in unity resisted any temptation to give it up and break the chain of commitment and communal loyalty.

In the end, we accepted the jungle's persistent punishment for having the gall to intrude upon its home. In addition to all else, the jungle took its pound of flesh from each of us by robbing a part of our soul, which we knew we'd never get back, at least not all of it, and certainly not the way it was.

But where is the enemy?

8

FOXTROT ECHO ALPHA ROMEO

> Keep your fears to yourself, but share
> your courage with others
> — Robert Louis Stevenson

Fear is the lifeblood of war. It is a weapon without bias, a powerful neutral force that can drive you mad or determine who lives or dies.

Before I landed in Vietnam at the ripe age of nineteen, I had never known fear, certainly not the kind that can throttle the heart and freeze the mind. The closest I suppose I ever got were jitters from competitive long-distance running, the anxiety runners feel in the normal course before the chase to victory begins.

Wartime fear was something else entirely.

Vietnam had an overriding fear, an omnipresent and menacing vibe in the deep background, always threatening to expand and cascade, like jungle winds suggestive of an impending storm.

Other times fear was situation specific, like when danger dropped in the path of a patrol without warning, filling your entire body with severe agitation. *Is it a good day to die?*

Well trained and with leadership who kept us honest, we were expected to ward off fear, to become its master, not the inverse. We could ill afford to succumb to its power.

Fear came in many forms, and not everyone experienced them all or in the same way. We each had our frailties and DNA markers. We couldn't expect everyone to handle the stress the same way. We had to compensate for one another.

No matter what anyone might say, the one fear everyone in Vietnam experienced, and some more often than others, was the fear of death—the ultimate price for being in the worst wrong place at the worst wrong time. Everyone felt it at one time or another because everyone knew it could happen any second, when you least expected it.

Fear of death was a shadow following us everywhere we went. You could ignore it most days. We had to. We couldn't function otherwise. But it never left. It patiently waited.

As a matter of military discipline, we were expected to push the fear of death out of our consciousness. If you dwelt on it, you were an instant liability. You endangered yourself, and, worse, you endangered others and worse still, jeopardized missions. Everyone understood that. We looked out for each other. We relied on each other to step up when the time came. So, while most didn't spend time fearing death, they might spend time fearing someone who did.

As a matter of mental sanity, keeping fear of death at bay was essential. The more you thought about it, the more unhinged you risked becoming. It could be an emotionally slippery slope if your mind began to weaken, allowing your imagination to run roughshod over your sensory powers. Gripped by fear, you might misinterpret jungle sounds or become preoccupied with the safety of a well-traveled trail or worry about the military soundness of a reconnaissance mission. As your mind went, so did your judgment and stability.

As if fear of death weren't enough, we had other fears to confront and conquer. Sometimes we feared sleep, concerned we might not hear the noise that brought our young lives to an abrupt end. Many worried about what they may never hear, as if waiting to die suddenly while awake and without notice somehow made it better. The truth was, death, if it decided to pay you a visit during the night, usually arrived before the noise that brought it. I learned early the vital importance of sleep. We exhausted ourselves on missions. We needed to rest to execute what we were sent to do. I wanted to sleep whenever I could. If it was my time to go over to the other side of Big Ridge, I would just as soon have it happen swiftly, when I least expected it, when I was happily dreaming of the normal things I planned to do when I got deposited back in The World. Let the lights go out in an instant, like the flipping of a switch on the wall. If it was to be, let me die in my sleep.

The most understandable fear was taking the life of another, someone you didn't know and would never know, someone who had done you no harm before, whose name you didn't know but was someone's young son like you. While some Marines were what the public might call gung-ho, primed to mow down the enemy given a chance, I wasn't crazy about the idea. But spend enough time in a war zone, witnessing death and maiming, experiencing others trying to kill you, receiving regular gruesome and devastating reports about activity in other parts of the country, and you begin to see killing as more natural, even normal, a perspective you never imagined you'd have.

And, as hard as it was to let that become part of you, the fear of killing could be what got you killed. It could freeze you at the precise moment you needed to act with extreme urgency to save your life and those of others. It had to be overcome.

Of course, it's easy to wax philosophical about such things far removed from the imminent dangers we faced in those times.

And, in fairness, we didn't normally obsess about them back then. If you let them simmer too long, they could bubble up into your throat and clog your mind. We didn't have time to contemplate our navel or draw on religious or moral bearings. It was either survive or die. For many, including me, killing became instinctive, much like the animals that inhabited the jungle we had invaded. The more time we spent in the jungle, the more like the local creatures we became.

Fear of death and killing had a counter side. We sometimes had to deal with fear of survival, of avoiding death, of having done our jobs well or gotten plain lucky. Survival sometimes meant someone else didn't. Why him? What did he do to deserve his fate? Why not me? What did I do to escape the call?

I think of all the fears I had in-country, the fear of survival gnawed at me the most, and not only the guilt part. I also feared surviving with less of me than I had when I arrived. Might I lose an eye or a limb? Might I wind up in a wheelchair for the rest of my life? Might I live but in a reconstituted physical or mental form with narrow boundaries around what I was able to do with my post-war existence? Would I become an object of pity or ridicule?

Vietnam brought a steady drumbeat of physical, emotional, and mental taxation. Sometimes it was subtle. Sometimes it pounded us hard. Over time, it became an accumulation of deprivation that wore us down to the bone, to the point where we could feel a breaking point approaching, and a different fear might set in, the fear of going insane or perhaps not insane, but, well, a little off and not quite right. We joked about losing it, could even be cavalier about it, but the joking masked an essential truth. We knew that any of us could go off the deep end. It might happen after a gradual, silent buildup. And then, without notice, the mind could snap, like what happened to that Marine in the latrine scene in *Full Metal Jacket*. One day he seemed okay. The next he was bonkers.

We knew human tolerance levels couldn't last indefinitely. I never saw it happen, but we heard the stories. I couldn't imagine what it must feel like to fear losing the mind, to know at some deep level, it is slipping away, and you are getting more untethered and isolated, living in a bubble of your own, and you can't stop it. How scary it must be.

The closest I got to that feeling was when hunkered down in an overnight position in the pitch-black jungle. The Vietnam jungle was so dark at night, you could wave your fingers in front of your nose and not see them. You'd hear noises all the time, most real, some unknown, and some imagined. Most times, the jungle sounds came from an animal moving about in its natural surroundings, living its life normally. But until you knew for sure, before you eliminated the other more threatening option in your mind, your heart stayed in your throat, and you began to get unsteady, teetering on the edge.

Fear of the unknown and fear of the next moment in utter darkness could fill every membrane in your body. The enemy favored nighttime movement, a time when our superior air support couldn't detect them. Any sound held the potential for them being in the vicinity, approaching with their signature stealth. They could swarm all over your team before you could breathe your next breath. Keeping it together in that situation, pushing the fear out of your throat, required a hold on mental stability, aware you could come face-to-face with the enemy any second and be overrun.

Sometimes in the still of the night, nothing seemed real or familiar. Time slowed down so much it became a collection of one eager breath after another over which I had no control, as if the brain were fighting a war against the rest of the body. Is that what it's like to go mad?

Then other times, the fear still there, I became robotic, a programmed fighting machine, not conscious of what I was doing, not feeling what I was doing, but still doing it, as I was programmed to do.

Then there were times when I understood where I was and what I was doing. I knew I had to stay focused and maintain control over my senses. I couldn't lose control. I had to be able to respond. I had to stay sharp. I couldn't lose the internal battle.

Those moments mirrored what I felt on patrol during the day whenever I sensed danger nearby. The daylight mitigated the suffocating feeling, but the rush of anxiety was fundamentally the same. As someone who walked point on patrol often, I had to be the eyes, ears, and sensory radar for the entire team. I often relied on instincts. After logging a handful of missions, I felt confident I could sense what was out there. Danger didn't always preview itself, but I could feel it, and with it came the fear of what might be coming.

The fear of impending trouble is powerful. But while I felt it, I didn't dwell on it. I had to switch to super-alert mode and regulate the pounding in my chest. My life and that of several others were in the balance. They counted on me. I embraced the role of point and didn't want anyone else to do it. But that didn't mean I didn't feel the fear of the moment. I had to demote my fear in favor of my sense of responsibility to my comrades.

Harder to shake was the fear that came with hanging from a ladder in the sky while a CH-46 dragged us out of the jungle to return us to base camp. Sometimes, choppers couldn't land to extract us at the end of a mission because, for example, the enemy was closing ranks behind us. We had to rappel (ascend) up a ladder, get strapped in, and hold on for our lives, hanging unprotected, while the chopper ascended into the sky and made its way back to Camp Reasoner. As we hung floating in the breeze, we were sitting ducks for any enemy within range. Until we got beyond enemy attack capability, we were at risk for our lives. It was fear born of helplessness.

But as my tour in-country crept closer to its end, I relaxed more. I started moving through missions virtually on autopilot. Others raised concerns. Was I getting sloppy? Had I lost my edge? Was I exposing others to greater risk? Was I losing my mind?

It wasn't as if I was winging it. I had become jungle and war comfortable, probably too much so. I had conquered most of my earlier fears. The concerns others expressed about me had some legitimacy, but not because I didn't care or wasn't paying attention to the cues, but because healthy doses of fear, which I no longer had, were needed to stay sharp. A residue of fear, it turned out, was essential to my job to stay on top of things, to be wary enough to be careful and exercise sound judgment and not be too confident.

Fear was the antidote for cockiness, which I had started to develop. The jungle had trained me well. I was fitting in, and while that was welcome at one level, for it made life more comfortable and tolerable, it could be dangerous too. I no longer had those internal butterflies that allowed me to have the caution necessary to do the job right. I didn't fear the prospects. I wanted contact with the enemy. Bring it on. I was beginning to enjoy it.

Looking back, I wonder whether, in a small way, I had gone a little insane. Becoming comfortable with war to the point you take things for granted and lose all sense of caution raises concerns about mental health, even if temporary. Fear had so dominated the landscape of our existence, I found getting free of fear invigorating, a release from the craziness. But maybe it was an entrée into madness.

* * *

When I became a short-timer, as the days ticked loudly off the calendar, and a military discharge came into view, I experienced a new fear.

I began to fear going home. I feared being treated like a pariah, that no matter what I had done or not done, I would be considered a baby-killer and destroyer of homes, families, and lives. I feared being the object of hate, shunned and isolated. No one would understand me, or they would feel uncomfortable in my presence. They'd rather I went away than try to understand me. And, if I didn't fit in, if I was ostracized or marginalized, I feared what life had in store for me.

Most of all, I feared what I may have become without understanding or even realizing the full impact of how the war had impacted me. I was always an easygoing, happy-go-lucky guy who enjoyed life with great zeal and enthusiasm. But now who was I? What had a tour of duty in Vietnam as a recon patrol member done to that nineteen-year-old kid from California? Who had the war made me? Deep down I knew I wasn't the same person. I just didn't know who that person was, and I feared finding out.

In some ways, the fear of coming home immobilized me more than anything I'd felt while in-country. Still, I don't ever want to underestimate the fears we faced each day in that war zone. It beat down the strongest of us. It disassembled the weakest. Most of us, and I for sure, hardened over time to those fears. I hope that was a good thing. I am still not sure.

— 9 —

DOC

> It is Doc's job to protect his brothers from Death,
> to knock him aside and say, "Not today."
> — Adam Fenner

Wartime quiet on the jungle trail can be shattered without warning, and, in a flash, your recon unit is in serious trouble. From hidden places, barrages of short rounds whizz past you pinging trees, thick brush, rocks, and dirt, and satchel charges explode here and there, ripping up the damp jungle floor while your recon unit gallantly returns fire in kind. The mixture of sounds can rattle you as smoke blurs sight lines, and your eyes burn with sweat. Weapon in hand, searching for a target, your head turns on a swivel, and your eyes dart all around. The shadows that drape the tree canopies, once seductive, now conceal the enemy, and you fear you might mistake one of yours for one of theirs. Your nerves are frayed, and adrenalin pumps your heart. You wonder if your patrol leader has called in artillery, and you hope against hope to hear the *chuff-chuff* sounds of an approaching CH-46 to provide cover and extract you. And then, you hear the dreaded plea piercing the madness: "Corpsman up!"

In the realm of Marine reconnaissance, there was probably no more valued member of the unit than the corpsman, the assigned medical support courtesy of the Navy, as the Marine Corps lacks its own medical division. The recon corpsman was the functional equivalent of the Army medic. To show utmost respect, we called him "Doc."

It is sometimes said that combat soldiers have three rules of war. Rule One: "Good men will die." Rule Two: "Not even Doc can change Rule One." And Rule Three: "Doc will die trying to change Rules One and Two." As a Marine once put it, the corpsman will "go through the gates of hell for one of their wounded Marines."

We are not talking about some silver-haired version of TV's Dr. Marcus Welby, or someone who has logged countless hours tending to civilian patients in well-equipped urban U.S. hospitals. We are talking, in the main, about kids, maybe twenty-one-years old, some slightly older, some slightly younger. Kids with minimal medical training, mostly on the job, shouldering incomprehensible responsibilities under horrendous conditions.

When on patrol, these wet-behind-the-ears youngsters knew that in any enemy engagement, they would likely hear that soul-shattering call, "Corpsman up," their cue to spur into action to provide emergency medical assistance, despite the risks to their own lives. It was their alarm bell to move with urgent speed to, for example, clear an airway filled with blood, stop profuse bleeding from a wound, perhaps an artery, treat for severe shock, administer bandages or splints, and otherwise care for the fallen—while the brutal sounds of war continued around them.

The corpsman was our true and steady first responder. We entrusted our lives to him each day on recon missions. We knew that no matter how terrible the situation, no matter how dire circumstances seemed, we could rest assured Doc was close by, watching and ready and motivated, that he always had our back—without exception. The corpsman was one of a kind.

We had an unspoken creed. Never let harm come to our corpsman, whatever it took. I never knew one Marine who wasn't willing to sacrifice his life for that of the corpsman. Recon patrol members bonded with each other like combat soldiers do, but the bond with Doc was different. That bond had an indestructible forever quality, with life and well-being delicately held in the balance.

He protected us and we protected him.

For our part, we weren't always successful. It was war, jungle war, a terrible, vicious kind of battle, where surprises cropped up and devastation reigned.

During the Vietnam War, 10,000 Navy corpsmen served with their Marine brothers, and of them 645 were killed in action and 3,300 wounded.

Corpsman enjoyed more leeway and less scrutiny than the rest of us. Boundaries for corpsman sometimes shifted, not that they engaged in flagrant flouting of rules, only that they got the benefit of the doubt more often than not. That was, mind you, no perk. Corpsmen were in short supply, and we could ill afford to lose one to some smartass lieutenant's misguided power play at discipline. Better one of us take the heat than allow our potential savior to get compromised.

Know this too. Corpsmen weren't insulated from the grind of battle. On the contrary. Knowing they could get pressed into grunt service, they wore two hats, supplementing their medical work with combat and tactical responsibilities. They cross-trained with the rest of us and had to be battle ready, and they came equipped for the challenge. In addition to a fully equipped medical bag, surgical kit, and other medical accoutrements like IV bottles, Ringer's lactate, morphine, and the painkilling Darvon, as well as extra canteens of water in the event of heatstroke, they carried an M16, magazines brimming with ammo, sometimes an M79 grenade launcher, and an inventory of grenades and smoke bombs. They may have been technically Navy, but in their heart and soul and bloodstream, they were Marines.

A corpsman often got called upon to make snap decisions in impossible situations. Should he, for example, administer morphine to relieve unbearable pain, or would the morphine be too much for the wounded Marine to handle, ending his life? If morphine was in short supply, how should Doc decide who among the wounded gets it and how much and who, possibly, gets none and must suffer the consequences of his judgment call? How easy is it to make such decisions when all around you AK-47 rounds are shattering the environment? How do you keep a clear head in that circumstance, a far cry from the relatively comfy confines of a field medical facility?

And then there was innovation, using techniques never taught but perhaps read about in a magazine, or imagined, like placing a hand into a gaping leg wound to apply and hold down a clamp to a severed artery to stem bleeding, without which death was sure to follow. The corpsman—again, probably barely old enough to order a beer in a bar or vote—often was what separated a wounded comrade from a deprived future.

I recall a specific encounter at the end of a mission when we were taking heavy fire, and I was running as fast as I could toward the extraction site and waiting chopper. Bullets whizzed past me while the chopper gunner sent rounds toward the enemy to provide us cover. As I approached the chopper, I saw the corpsman running in the opposite direction in the face of enemy fire to assist a downed Marine. Who does that?

Sometimes corpsmen faced moral dilemmas. One, for example, came upon a local villager packed with shrapnel and losing blood. If left without medical assistance, death was certain. But when Doc called for a medevac chopper to move her to a field hospital for medical treatment, his superiors denied the request, explaining that emergency responses for civilians were taboo and ordered him to leave the girl and move on. Faced with obeying an order or trying to save a life, the corpsman chose life. He put the young woman on an IV, disinfected, dressed, and bandaged her wounds, administered a modest dose of morphine, and, not the least, kept her company. Eventually, the powers that be caved, and she got medevacked, and by the grace of deserved luck, the Doc avoided a court martial for disobeying orders. The girl lived.

Corpsmen in recon were truly their brothers' keepers. They were selflessly committed to saving lives and, in the face of devastation, providing hope. Because of them, we got another breath and another day. They always had to be ready, and ready they always were.

— 10 —

TUN TAVERN

> A Marine is a Marine... there's no
> such thing as a former Marine.
> — General James F. Amos, USMC (Ret.)

One at a time, seconds and minutes apart, each member of our recon patrol team strolled into the Staggerback Inn, the prized watering hole at Camp Reasoner built by Delta Company and located between company headquarters and our hooch.

The gathering was a long-honored tradition. The night before a recon mission, the team assembled for a cold beer or two, each member knowing but no one saying it could be the last beers they might enjoy.

Staggerback Inn was special, the lone meeting place at Camp Reasoner for enlisted men—and normally enlisted men only—to enjoy brew, listen to music together, and simulate a home environment and a sense of normal. The energy and vibe in Staggerback were day-to-day upbeat. An oasis of a different kind.

As structures go, it was primitive. Raised from the ground on short stump posts, its exterior sported plywood walls painted green and a pitched aluminum roof. A makeshift plywood sign announced the venue with a brown background and three stacked words painted white, "Stagger, Back, Inn," next to which someone painted a cartoonish military figure that could have been found in the Beetle Bailey regiment. Stenciled on the outside wall by year was the name of each Marine from the battalion KIA.

Inside the Staggerback Inn were scattered a handful of tables with green plastic tablecloths set against the background of a nondescript counter. Some ornaments hung from the ceiling; pictures were on the walls, and war trophies took up space around the inside perimeter. Artwork sometimes appeared in the time-honored sculptured form of empty beer can pyramids. It had a few windows. Otherwise, the place was Spartan, occupying about 1,500 square feet.

Unless your entire patrol found themselves in Staggerback at the same time, in which case you collected as a group, subcultures segregated about—Blacks, Hispanics, rednecks, white Easterners, and stragglers from California. Despite the segregation, controversy had no place.

On busy nights behind the counter, you'd find a makeshift bartender to serve beer. Other nights, we were relegated to self-service. Music blared, always, and first come, first choice determined the genre, country versus Motown versus jazz versus rock and roll, the latter often derided as "hippie music." Whatever the chosen sound on any given night, decibels were dialed up.

The most popular and cherished feature of Staggerback was its simplest: cold beer in a can, a luxury in the jungle. Washing a cold one down a parched throat after several days in the godforsaken Vietnam jungle unleashed every sensory nerve and uplifted the soul.

* * *

During the morning of Tuesday, November 9, 1970, my patrol leader and I received a briefing on a dangerous recon mission to start the next day. In the afternoon, the entire unit had a warm meal, and that night we gathered at the Staggerback Inn for beers and small talk.

"You know what tomorrow is, right?" said Lieutenant Michael Capers, our patrol leader.

"The next day of my life?" said Lance Corporal Jake Smale, primary radioman.

"Ah, indeed, that for sure. But what else?"

"It's goddamn November 10th."

"Bingo," said Capers.

"So?" said Smale.

"So? It's an important birthday."

Everyone looked around the table. Some shrugged. No one spoke.

"Okay, sir, did we forget your birthday?" said Smale.

"No, my fellow leathernecks, it's *our* birthday tomorrow."

Everyone smiled and looked around the table in search of a clue. Capers laughed to himself, shook his head, and picked up where he left off.

"Tomorrow, November 10th, the first day of our next mission, which we will execute proudly and well, is the birthday of the United States Marines Corps."

A few "wows" hit the air. "Here, here," someone said.

"You guys ever heard of Tun Tavern?" said Capers.

After a few seconds of silence, Justin Ingram, the unit's corpsman, looked to see if anyone was going to respond, and seeing no one, said, "Actually, um, sir, I have."

"Enlighten your uninformed comrades a little, Doc."

"Well, here's what I remember. In, I believe it was, 1685, a Philadelphia businessman—"

"Name's Samuel Carpenter," Capers interjected.

"Yes, yes, that's it. Anyway, this guy Carpenter started a brew house on the Philadelphia waterfront off a street named Tun Alley, the first of its kind in the city, and he called it Tun Tavern."

"Sooo?" said Wally Packard, our rifleman.

"So, it later became a famous meeting place that had some connection to how the Marines got started," said Doc Ingram.

"Doc, do you know the historical details?" said Capers.

"Not sure, sir. I think I'll defer to you there."

"Fair enough. Listen up, men."

"Carpenter had this idea that Tun Tavern could be the cornerstone of commercial development for the Philadelphia waterfront. He knew his shit, it turns out, because, sure enough, word spread rapidly, and Tun Tavern became a hub for people to gather and drink beer."

"Kind of like Staggerback Inn, eh sir?" said Ingram.

"Precisely, Doc."

"In time, Tun Tavern became the central meeting place for city and colonial officials and, eventually, revolutionaries."

"Revolutionaries? As in the American Revolution?" said PFC Rich Ripley, our tail-end Charlie.

"Yup, them revolutionaries," said Capers.

"Tun Tavern later added a restaurant, Peggy Mullan's Red Hot Beef Steak Club—remember that—and in the 1740s, our Founding Fathers began to eat and meet there."

"Hey, Lieutenant, I wonder if the food was as good as what we get in Reasoner," said Ripley.

"Ha, good thought. We can all agree we are fortunate to have quality meals here, no longer a well-kept secret. Maybe the Reasoner chefs got their hands on Ms. Mullan's recipes."

Capers took a long pull of his beer, emptying the can, and popped open another before continuing. Others did the same and returned their attention to him. He had a rapt audience.

"You'll appreciate this next tidbit, men ... In 1756, none other than Benjamin Franklin organized the Pennsylvania Militia and used Tun Tavern to recruit its soldiers to respond to disputes with Native Americans. Then, in the 1770s, the Continental Congress convened at Tun Tavern to plan next steps in their escalating dispute with the British Crown."

"Damn, Tun Tavern was a badass place," said Smale.

"It was, and the best is yet to come," said Capers.

"In late 1774, John Adams—I assume you all remember him—led a seven-person committee at Tun Tavern in drafting articles of war and commissioning a new naval fleet."

"Serious business," said Smale.

"Then, on November 10, 1775—always remember that date—the Continental Congress assigned a local innkeeper, Samuel Nicholas, to raise the first two battalions of Marines, appointing him captain and commandant of the new Continental Marines. They also labeled Robert Mullan, son of Peggy Mullan—the woman I mentioned earlier with the Tun Tavern restaurant—as chief marine recruiter.

Capers took a sip of beer.

"Using a Conestoga wagon outside the Tun Tavern, Nicholas and the younger Mullan recruited skilled marksmen to become the first Marines, a company consisting of 100 Rhode Islanders. They were posted aboard Continental Navy ships."

"And that, gentlemen, is why Tun Tavern is considered the birthplace of the United States Marine Corps, and it happened on November 10th."

"Is that how the Corps became part of the Navy, sir?" said Ripley.

"I believe so. Speaking of which, let me share a related legendary story," said Capers.

"Remember John Paul Jones?"

"Yes, the 'I've not yet begun to fight' dude, right?" said J. T. Anderson, our secondary radioman.

"The one and the same," said Capers.

"Jones captained what is considered one of the most memorable maritime war engagements in U.S. Navy history, a four-hour battle against the British in the Revolutionary War. His major allies? None other than 137 Marines who served with Jones on his ship. They were called the "Wild Geese," and most were Irish exiles. Victory was at hand when a Marine tossed a grenade that set the rival British ship on fire. During that battle, Jones uttered those famous words."

Packard asked, "Lieutenant, what about the term *leathernecks*? Did that start with Tun Tavern?"

"Good question. No, I don't think so. There is confusion about its origins. Some say that the Marines began wearing a leather neckband as protection from sword slashes to the throat during the Revolutionary War. Others say it was a uniform design to achieve discipline, to keep heads up and eyes straight.

"And my point man, Corporal Walton, you've been silent the whole time. Where is that normally inquisitive mind of yours?"

"The birthday thing is amazing. But I keep focusing on something else, that this is what we do before a mission, drinking and bullshitting, getting our minds right to do our job and possibly engage the enemy, just like the first Marines did over two hundred years ago in the American Revolution. Things haven't changed," I said. "Like us, they convened at a bar and had conversation and debate and, like us, got ready for battle over cold beers. We are privileged to stand in their boots. It's humbling and inspiring."

"Incredible, isn't it?" said Capers.

"It truly is," I said.

Lt. Capers lifted his can of beer to the middle of the table. Everyone else did the same.

"Gentlemen," Capers said, "here's to the Corps, to a successful mission, and to us . . . that, God willing, we each shall return to this very spot in five days for another cold one. Semper fi."

"Semper fi!" the unit said in unison.

The patrol ambled out of Staggerback Inn in single file and silence, like a recon patrol unit snaking through the bush, each member slave to private thoughts about what lay ahead. No more frivolity and friendly jousting. No more history lessons. It was game time with high stakes, like what the original Marines faced with bravery and loyalty to cause.

Will we all get to drink another beer?

Staggerback Inn

Gearing up for a mission in Staggerback Inn ala Tun Tavern

⬤ 11 ⬤

THE DECISION

> They were prepared to die for each other; more important, they were prepared to kill for each other.
> — Stephen Ambrose, *Band of Brothers*

When word of the unusual directive made its way to me, I knew something different was in store. Our military intelligence superiors (Intel) had commanded our entire patrol team to gather at HQ for a briefing on a new reconnaissance mission. In my experience, Intel limited mission briefings to the patrol leader, sometimes with the assistant patrol leader, who, in turn, briefed the rest of the recon team.

When I walked into the meeting room, I didn't recognize the officers seated at the table. Two were first lieutenants, the other a captain. The atmosphere was military somber. After customary salutes, we took our seats across the table as directed. I scanned the room. The stack of reports, various maps, aerial photos, and two notebooks on the table were quite the assortment. Yes, this had a different feel.

One first lieutenant did most of the talking. We were being sent to a location up north, about twenty miles inside enemy lines. We spent time with the maps and aerial photos. I had never been to the area. Nor, as it turned out, had any of the patrol team.

He told us matter-of-factly that the target location was beyond where artillery support could be given. I waited for him to add, "on the remote chance you might need it." He didn't.

Our mission was to infiltrate an enemy compound, a "staging camp," tucked away in a well-concealed jungle ravine, depicted in grainy photos. Once there, we were to kidnap two high-ranking officers, grab what documents we could, and hightail it out of there. By the sounds of it, this would be my most dangerous patrol to date. Mixed feelings of excitement and fear filled me.

Taking turns, the two lieutenants meticulously described the trails and terrain we were expected to use and repeatedly examined entry and escape routes from the staging camp. We looked at trail distances and assessed klicks in the grid for timing and distance and what was presumed safest among available trails. We reviewed the specified landing zones for chopper insertion and extraction and anticipated coordination with chopper pilots at both ends of the mission, and we discussed the likely impact of weather. They sometimes repeated parts of the briefing, pausing to make sure they had our rapt attention. They did.

At one point, in a rare intervention, the captain said, "You'll have no margin for error once you get to the camp—zero, absolutely none."

Unlike protocol in prior briefings, they reviewed each of our roles and what was specifically expected of us. They told us what to carry for food—one meal a day—how much water we could take, and the weaponry we each were to bring. They left little of the preparation to our discretion.

I was assigned the role of rifleman. In addition to being ready to engage in combat, I was to provide strategic support for our two team leaders, Lt. Butler and Sgt. Jacobson. I was also tasked with supporting the radiomen, helping them with navigation and radio codes.

I don't recall how long the briefing lasted, but it was longer than any I'd experienced.

At its conclusion, the captain rose and said, "Understood gentlemen?" While we all stood in unison and nodded, we knew he wasn't asking if we comprehended the substance of the briefing. The tone of his question conveyed what his eyes showed: *Each of you may die on this mission—understood?*

After salutes all around, they dismissed us with two days to get our minds right and prepare what they decreed was a maximum five-day mission. We each scattered to do our own thing until departure time.

I felt uneasy about the whole thing. I had questions I normally didn't have. Despite the exhaustive briefing, I wondered whether they'd left anything out, something they knew but didn't reveal to us, that if known might trigger doubt in the mission or increase trepidation. The briefing had that kind of feel. Also, what would happen if we got captured? And did they mean literally *no* artillery support, or was there a hidden message there as well?

Those questions would remain unanswered. Military brass didn't dabble in explanations. They told you what to do, and you did it.

I learned before we left that in advance of the briefing Lt. Butler had conferred with Intel, and, in concert with them and subject to their approval, had handpicked the team for this mission. The selection was assignment specific, a customized, one-time elite team. I suppose I should have been flattered, but getting selected for this was a far cry from getting voted onto the major league baseball all-star team. It was, at best, a dubious distinction.

I had never worked with Lt. Butler before, but he seemed a solid choice. He had a reputation that preceded him. He was short with a gymnast's body. He didn't smile much. A tough, seasoned Marine, he had logged many difficult missions and commanded respect. I took some comfort knowing we were in his good hands, although word was that when Lt. Butler led a patrol, enemy engagement often followed. He had a little bit of John Wayne in him, a part of his reputation that didn't inspire me.

The rifleman role, in honesty, took me aback. I was a seasoned recon Marine and accomplished point man and assistant patrol leader. It felt at first like a demotion. But I knew this was a cherry-picked team from a large population. Lt. Butler slated Sgt. Jacobson for the point instead. I had worked with Jacobson on several missions. The guy was tough as nails, an inspirational team leader, and as good a point as the corps could boast. Taller than the rest of us, he was in incredible condition. I couldn't complain.

Butler filled out the team with the customary spots: two radiomen, a corpsman, and a tail-end Charlie. On the trails, Sgt. Jacobson would lead the way, followed by Lt. Butler, the primary radioman, then me, followed by the corpsman, the second radioman, and the tail-end Charlie protecting our rear. I didn't know the others, other than by name and face.

DAY 1

Less than forty-eight hours after the briefing, at 4:30 a.m., we were set to go. Everyone was awake, packed, and geared up. Some were putting the final touches of camouflage to their faces, a time-honored ritual, the recon version of war paint. We squeezed black and green glops of camouflage goo out of silver tubes and mixed them with a generous dollop of jungle juice. The combination created a paste that, with the aid of personal hand mirrors, we dabbed onto our faces, using what creativity we could muster to design a customized pattern. It was as if we were getting ready for Halloween.

Artwork aside, the face mask provided jungle cover and anti-reflection from the sun and, thanks to the bug repellant, helped ward off mosquitoes.

As we walked to the takeoff spot, LZ 401, we could see our transportation, a CH-46, sitting stately against a backdrop of deep orange ripples revealing a rising sun. Despite the early hour, the atmosphere was drenched with humidity.

Nearing the chopper, we became engulfed with the delightful fragrance of diesel fumes and the pulsating sounds of a swirling chopper rotor. We had to scream at each other to be heard.

The chopper crew didn't look at us. They almost never did. It was as if they did not want to have images of breathing faces in case some returned without life in them. We didn't look at them either. The feeling, I guess, was mutual.

We double-checked our gear and weaponry. We briefly reviewed the maps and radio codes, weather reports, and compound entry and escape routes. We understood the meaning of "no margin for error."

We boarded the chopper, taking seats in the back section in collective silence. Except for a businesslike nod from Lt. Butler, none of us acknowledged the chopper personnel or the pilot, copilot, and two gunners. Eyes straight ahead, a gunner on the right flashed a thumbs-up to Lt. Butler, who signaled the same to the pilot, meaning it was a green light to go. The chopper ascended into the dawn sky, spraying dust everywhere.

Once above the tree lines, we were treated to splendid views of rice paddies, rivers, streams, fields, and the distant mountain ridges. Time passed in tranquil silence. I favored this part of recon patrols. It was always peaceful, a true quiet before the storm. We were safe at peak altitudes, where the enemy lacked the artillery firepower to cause us trouble. Until descension toward the LZ, the chopper ride was a Sunday stroll among the clouds.

Lack of eye contact dominated the flight. The team seemed more jittery than usual, even nervous, at this point of a mission. Their vibe confirmed my own ominous feelings about the mission. I wondered what each of them felt and thought. I dared not ask.

We began to approach deep valleys, and the landscape changed dramatically. Now we gazed at rolling, steep, foliage-filled mountains and thick, congested jungle terrain. I grabbed the map, assessed the coordinates and locations, and nodded to myself in recognition that we were nearing the LZ. Of course, the map couldn't reveal whether the LZ was safe. Intel presumed it was safe, or so they said. It didn't matter since a landing zone presumed safe could wind up being anything but safe upon arrival. In an instant, it could become the sight of a hostile engagement. No matter how good the intelligence, one thing was indisputable: once we began the descent toward the LZ, we were an easy target for small arms and mortar fire. That is why, on cue, as soon as we made our descent, tension inside the back of the chopper ratcheted up a notch or two.

When the LZ was in our sights, the chopper didn't zoom straight down as would normally happen. Instead, the pilot turned away from the target site and began to circle the ridge below. I didn't sense danger on the ground, but when the pilot circled again, I concluded his concern was the tree stands. He was searching for a wide enough opening in the trees to fly through. A landing zone might look clean from a distance, but on closer inspection can reveal tree configurations and growth that make it difficult or impossible to penetrate safely. If the pilot couldn't get us in, we'd likely have to rappel from a ladder in the sky, rendering us target practice should the enemy be nearby. Thankfully, the pilot deftly brought the bird through an opening he'd found and put us down smoothly in the middle of a robust pile of elephant grass.

We disembarked and immediately created a protective perimeter. In a flash, the chopper rose and left us. I watched it get smaller and smaller against the blue sky. The smaller it became, the lower the sound of the *whup-whup-whup* of its rotor—a gloomy reminder that we seven Marines were now alone, isolated on the outskirts of the jungle.

When the chopper dissolved into the sky, all became quiet. We sat there, inside our makeshift perimeter, beginning to feel the heat. Flying in the chopper gave us a much-appreciated break from the jungle's stifling air. But once we were boots on the ground, we felt the full power of the heat. I got used to many things in the jungle but never the unyielding heat. Jungle heat steals your breath, zaps your strength, and softens your mind.

As we readied to pound the turf, we listened to anything we could hear. We were now mindful of noises that might indicate the enemy was in dangerous proximity. We keyed to the ever-present possibility of an ambush from the ground, including the possibility of booby traps hidden below our feet, or a sniper attack from above. Our senses were on high alert.

That first day was uneventful. We traveled according to plan, humping terrain for a few hours. We made our way to a ridge top where we found good coverage amid a batch of trees. Lt. Butler decided to call it a day. We had made decent progress, but the heat was kicking our asses. We set claymore mines around the perimeter, established radio contact, had some food, such as it was, and eased into the night for needed sleep. We each had an hour of "radio watch," taking turns reporting to HQ via verbal whispers or clicks, letting them know our status.

DAY 2

The next morning, I joined Lt. Butler and Sgt. Jacobson for a quick huddle. We spoke in low whispers. It gave me an opportunity to see how they handled each other. I knew well that our fate could turn on the interpersonal dynamics between the patrol leader and second in command. Their mutual respect, camaraderie, and trust in each other counted for a lot, especially if we found ourselves in tricky circumstances. From what I could tell, Butler and Jacobson got on well and seemed to like each other, which boosted my confidence.

That said, and meaning no disrespect, I still wasn't comfortable with the others, at least not yet. I hadn't worked with them, and when sensing their nerves earlier, I began to have concerns, at least enough to be wary. I drew some comfort knowing that Lt. Butler had chosen each of them—as he did me—and that counted for something. Still, I had gotten to where I didn't take anything for granted in this jungle war. Show me, don't tell me. My cherished life could be in the balance.

As we got rolling the second day, traversing ridges, we tried to stay under cover as best we could, but now and then we slipped into the wide open to maintain progress and keep the prescribed schedule. Whenever that happened, we'd increase the distance between each of us to manage risk better—and hope for the best. After a couple of hours, we were deep within enemy territory, knowing the NVA could pay us a visit at any time.

The closer we got to our destination, the more focused I became. Although the heat was unbearable, we had to put it out of our minds, stay alert, and be ready for anything. Despite how much I was dialed in, I had to admit to some nerves. When your life is on the line, when you could literally be dead in a matter of seconds, you can normalize some degree of nervousness, so long as it doesn't impede your ability to do your job.

Thanks to our lucky stars, nothing of note happened that first full day on the trail, and when night approached, Lt. Butler ended our forward movement, and we settled in for the duration. As we always did, we first created our perimeter and laid out the claymores, keeping hushed tones. When nightfall arrived, we tried to get as much sleep as we could. I laid awake at first, straining to interpret the jungle sounds. They eventually relaxed me, and I dozed off.

DAY 3

It didn't happen often, but I got a good night's sleep. When I awoke, I was itching to get started. I felt a surge of energy and purpose. As the day unfolded, I could feel the adrenalin coursing through my body. I had to manage the vibe.

We continued along the same ridge line. The trail got wider and was in better condition than what we came across the first two days. Several arteries intersected the trail as we pushed deeper into the triple-canopy portion of the jungle. No question, the trails weren't virgin. We were getting close, and the chances of spotting the enemy excellent.

I wondered whether we should opt for a different ridge trail, off the beaten path, slower but safer. The more we were on the current trail, the more evidence of prior traffic we saw. The increased danger was obvious. On the other hand, we had two days to complete the mission, and going off the trail would cost precious time, as well as deplete food and water supplies. Tough call.

After whispered debate, we elected to stay where we were and take our chances rather than take a safer route and prolong the mission.

What seemed like only minutes later, Sgt. Jacobson, in the point position, stopped suddenly and thrust his arm into the air, the signal to freeze. Luckily, a bomb crater was nearby, and Lt. Butler directed the rest of us to jump in the crater and create a perimeter. The jungle terrain gave added buffer.

Lt. Butler joined Sgt. Jacobson while we waited. Less than thirty seconds later, we heard a cluster of shots ring out and seconds after that another short volley, all from M16s. It turned out that a Vietnamese man in white pajamas, carrying a weapon across his chest and a sack full of rice on his back had crossed our path. The first shots wounded him; the next barrage took him out. After depositing his body in the bushes, we resumed walking the trail. Minutes later, another Vietnamese crossed our path, he too in all white, with a weapon in hand and a rich supply of rice on his back. We shot and felled him as well, leaving his body in the bushes.

The two incidents took less than ten minutes each. While running into the enemy was of course no surprise, the incidents were enough to send a chill down my spine. And while we each maintained our poker faces, I am betting everyone, as I did, felt electricity in every membrane of their bodies.

We kept on and, miraculously, avoided further trouble. We selected another well-covered area, built our perimeter, and hunkered down for the night. We had been lucky up until this point. I wondered whether we had any luck left in our arsenal. We likely would need it.

DAY 4

The next morning, I rose, got my act together for the day's festivities, and found a private place to sit to gather myself. Perched on the ridge, I watched the sun rise. It was a large ball throwing off hues of ruby red and burnt orange through the thin cloud cover. Absolutely magnificent. In the distance, though, some of the mountain ridges were shrouded in thick gray fog and low dark clouds, suggesting rain might be in our near future, despite the absence of winds that normally foreshadowed a downpour. I tried to draw some meaning from the contrast in the two vistas, some message from the universe to preview what was to come, but nothing dropped my way. I was eager to get on with it.

Lt. Butler collected us and, in a whisper, said we were headed into a steep canyon off the trail through dense triple-canopy jungle. It would take us to our destination and the planned rendezvous with the enemy. He eyeballed us, nodded to Sgt. Jacobson, and off we went down the trail.

It was tough going. The cliffs were steep, slippery, and rocky. We struggled to keep our balance. Once in the thick of the jungle, the humidity began choking us. It was sticky wet. Worse, while it getting close to noon, the jungle was middle-of-the-night dark, except for occasional shards of sunlight that slithered through seams in the tree canopies, forming tiny blotches of light on the jungle floor, like a super flashlight beamed from above.

We also battled clusters of wait-a-minute vines that abused us, grabbing and tossing us around, sticking us with needles, and ripping our clothes. It was the absolute worst of the jungle. The sole saving grace was the decent coverage from above that the density offered.

After an unbearably slow four- to five-hour grind, we still hadn't struck pay dirt. Lt. Butler held us up to catch our breath. Checking the map, I could see we were within striking distance. Lt. Butler suggested we hunker down and complete the mission first thing in the morning. It was debatable. We were *so* close. The compound residents were likely in a laid-back mode. We had the element of surprise as night approached, which also should help us circumvent perimeter sentries. On the other hand, the waning visibility could work both ways, maybe even favor the enemy. And the element of surprise might be as good in the morning if not better.

The more I thought about it, waiting until morning made the most sense. We were depleted, and some sleep, even fitful, would replenish our strength somewhat. The morning seemed a good time to get our minds right and refocus more effectively on the endgame. And that is what we elected to do.

DAY 5

The rains visited us during the night but nothing too turbulent or cold. I think I slept okay but honestly don't recall. In the morning, I prepared a meal, repainted my face, and got ready. The decision to stay another night before executing the mission was wise. Everyone seemed relatively fresh and in good spirits.

We had a difficult trek awaiting us. Four hundred meters doesn't sound like much. But dragging our butts and gear down steep, rocky, wet jungle terrain with monstrous growth all around in a lightless jungle can happen only at a snail's pace. We crawled over boulders, slipped on muddy rocks and broken branches, and tripped on roots, trying to maintain balance and be quiet at the same time. Each step was part art and part science.

We weren't down the canyon thirty minutes when we began to smell smoke and fish and rice cooking and the musky, almost pleasant scent, of elephant dung. The farther we went, the more light the jungle gave us. We even got a cool breeze from the mountain, which mitigated the brutal humidity. Thousands of ants moved in parallel with us along the trail at our feet. The closer we got to the camp, the more birds we saw sweeping down from the trees. The jungle was breathing signs of life.

My senses intensified, and my back muscles tightened under the strain of my sixty-pound pack. I knew I couldn't allow the discomfort to throw my focus or move me off balance. Efficiency depended on each of us moving in near lockstep and maintaining rhythm, no matter what the obstacles. We were about to engage the enemy.

I strained my ears to hear evidence of enemy activity. I heard nothing. Then, we saw two enemy sentries maintaining a post way off to the side of where we were. They seemed distracted and had no clue about our presence. They were lounging around smoking cigarettes. The early morning hour seemed to have compromised their acute sense of attention. Whatever the reason, they were being sloppy.

Beyond them we could see the full compound at the ravine bottom. Wow.

We didn't see any life mulling in the open areas of the camp. Moving continuously with stealth, we slipped undetected past the perimeter section where the guards were lounging around, aided in part by steam rising from the jungle floor that shielded us from visual detection. We could now see all the huts and shacks and living quarters. It was a small, well-maintained village. I estimated forty to sixty military personnel, upward of eight times our team. Quaint and cozy, the village was well isolated from civilization, which in the moment favored us, as its habitants likely were groggy-headed and nonchalantly easing into the day.

A nearby stream flowed under a short bridge, which invited us to cross, and we did. Once on the other side, we could see the officers' hooch, prominently situated in the rear middle of the camp. Our destination was in our sight lines. It was time to execute.

I was tasked with providing cover for Lt. Butler and Sgt. Jacobson as they went to snatch our targets from the hooch. The rest of our team set up a perimeter and kept close tabs on the escape route. Our radiomen contacted HQ with an update. We got out the tape, blindfolds, and rope to restrain the snatched prisoners. Lt. Butler and Sgt. Jacobson removed their packs. They had no more than one minute, and likely less, to get across the compound, enter the hooch, grab the two officers and what papers they could, and return to us, relying mainly on the element of surprise.

They were off, moving like cats across the compound. As they did, I scanned the rest of the compound for evidence of additional guards or any trouble. I didn't see any. I knew that wouldn't last long.

As Butler and Jacobson approached the hooch, I heard my heart pounding against the inner wall of my chest. In all my time in Vietnam, in all the situations that had triggered fear or severe anxiety in me, I'd never heard my heart pound like that. It hurt. My eyes widened. My jaw clenched. My hands tightened their grip on my M79. I could feel small beads of sweat forming on my forehead. I was exploding with adrenaline.

Then, Butler and Jacobson disappeared into the hooch. I held my breath and didn't want to let it out until I saw them again, alive and well, with prisoners in tow.

Seconds later, Lt. Butler and Sgt. Jacobson emerged from the hooch, rifles trained on two prisoners, charging ahead with urgency. One of the two, I don't recall who, held a batch of confiscated documents. I kept my eyes trained on the hooch and the nearby vicinity for a possible retaliatory attack. It seemed like an eternity, but they reached us in less than thirty seconds. It was surreal. I was shaking a little.

We had work to do, and we had to do it fast. We secured the prisoners and placed them in front of the tail-end Charlie, so if we got attacked, they'd be more exposed than most of us. Everyone was focused. We assembled ourselves with precision and efficiency and hit the trail with the two restrained prisoners. So far, the Intel plan had worked as designed.

Before the good feeling about execution had a chance to subside, however, we came under fire. As shots rang out, we kept moving, struggling out of the ravine in the direction of the high ridge. Lt. Butler and Sgt. Jacobson began to return the volley, and we joined them in what now was a distant firefight. The limited numbers that came after us weren't prepared for a full-out skirmish. We had indeed surprised them, and they dared not enter the fray too deeply without reinforcements. They had no idea of our size or capability at that point. But that wouldn't last long. They stopped firing, and we broke contact and ran up the steep trail, forcing the prisoners to move at a hurried pace, not looking back, hoping everyone was okay. We got to a lower ridge, in a protective spot, not knowing how much time we had, and regrouped. We took a head count. Everyone seemed okay. We had scrapes and cuts from the hastiness of the retreat but otherwise were fine.

We knew we weren't out of the woods yet, and they'd come after us in significantly greater numbers. So, once we knew everyone was okay, we prepared to resume the climb. Before doing so, however, we discovered a significant problem. In the brief firefight, the NVA had hit one of the prisoners, a dose of friendly fire. He took rounds in the shoulder, arm, and hand. While bleeding profusely, he wasn't critical.

We couldn't leave him. He was an asset that we'd been directed to bring back. Further, leaving him would expose us, since he could reconnect with his comrades and tell them our size, weaponry, most recent whereabouts, and presumed route. On the other hand, he would slow us down, especially on the steep climb we faced. At the slowed pace he'd force us to take, even if we got to the higher ridge, we had to assume the NVA would likely catch us at some point.

For the time being, though, we decided to bring him with us, which meant carrying him as we labored to gain more separation from the enemy.

When we got to a bomb crater, we stopped to rest. Everyone was breathing hard. Thin layers of fear had shadowed many faces. No one said what we all presumably thought, that at the current pace we could be dead within the hour. Each second we weren't moving brought us closer to that fate.

Lt. Butler, Sgt. Jacobson, and I separated from the rest of the team to discuss the situation. Lt. Butler asked the corpsman to join the summit. I was soon to learn why.

I thought we could make it to the landing zone with the wounded prisoner. Lt. Butler was doubtful, or at least disinclined to chance it. He asked the corpsman if he had enough morphine to overdose the prisoner. The corpsman asked how much time before we likely were overrun. Butler said soon if we don't get rid of the prisoner. The corpsman resisted. He didn't want to sacrifice any morphine, concerned that patrol members, who were his primary responsibility, might need some, sooner rather than later. They went back and forth. The corpsman was firm in his stance, doubtlessly pondering the possibility of disobeying a direct order if Lt. Butler directed him to inject a fatal dose of morphine into the prisoner. For his part, Lt. Butler had to consider the consequences of issuing an order of that nature. We were in crisis mode.

Lt. Butler took the morphine idea off the table. We had expended two to three precious minutes figuring that out.

The other option was to shoot the prisoner. But the risk there was plain and unacceptable. Firing rounds would give away our position and defeat the purpose. Both sides knew the sounds of each other's weapons like the backs of their hands. The sound of a fired M16, or a .45 pistol for that matter, pinpointed location. It would be like signing our death warrants.

Lt. Butler and Sgt. Jacobson agreed we had to off the wounded prisoner, but quietly. I didn't have a vote, although it was hard to argue with the reasoning. If we didn't off him and dragged him with us or left him as is, either way, we likely would be overrun and get massacred. We lacked the battle resources of the enemy. We saw the size of the compound. We could do the math. One way or the other, we were as good as dead.

Killing him quietly gave us the only practical chance of survival.

Butler decided we had to kill the wounded prisoner with a Ka-Bar, our standard-issue knife. We shielded the other prisoner to block his vision. The wounded prisoner knew immediately what was about to happen. The fear in his eyes was riveting. It was like nothing I'd ever seen or ever wanted to see again. It sent me into a dark, disgusting place.

We laid the wounded prisoner on his back in the crater, his hands tied, and put a makeshift mask over his face. Sgt. Jacobson grabbed his head, pushed it back, and began to stab him in the chest. As he did, the prisoner fought for his life, rolling over and trying to get up. Less than a minute later, the prisoner was still alive, and Butler became impatient. He waived off Sgt. Jacobson and took the knife. He directed me to pull the head of the prisoner back, put a knee in his back, and hold him down. The mask had fallen to the ground from all the writhing. The prisoner was turning to look at me with begging and helpless eyes. I couldn't look at him and turned way. When I pulled his head back, Butler slashed his throat. The resulting sounds were so revolting, I instinctively looked to see.

Blood gushed from his throat like a water sprinkler all over his chest. The knife didn't penetrate easily. Lt. Butler struggled to make it work. It became haphazard. Blood began to shoot everywhere. Panic set in. I had trouble breathing. My vision got blurry. We couldn't stay much longer. We had to get moving. Lt. Butler wasn't finished. The prisoner was choking on his own blood and struggling to live. His neck was swelling up with blood, and he started making loud gurgling sounds. It was insane. He was fighting the inevitability of death. We had to go. We rifled through this uniform, finding letters and a picture of his wife and children. We were, in the moment of that discovery, the same as him. We dumped him in the mud and covered him lightly with dirt. He lay still, dying. We quickly reassembled and left.

After that, I have no clue what happened. None. Try as I might, I cannot remember anything else of that day, what I assume was our final day on patrol. We made it back to the extraction site, an LZ that presumably Intel had set up for us close by, along with perhaps two potential extraction sites to hedge bets, but I don't know what it was like getting there. We were extracted by a CH-46 presumably, but I have no memory of boarding a helicopter or riding back. I also don't recall discussing with anyone what happened with the prisoner, never mind the details. After leaving the prisoner, my mind is a complete blank.

I have tried to recall those things. I wanted to know how I processed what happened, and how others did. How did I feel then? How did they feel? What thoughts did they have once the dust settled? What were mine? But I can't call up any of it, no matter how hard I try.

As much as I wish to remember the aftermath, I want to forget what I do remember, all that blood, so much blood. I want to excise from my mind the image of the terrified eyes of a young man we had to kill brutally so the seven of us could live another day. I want to cleanse my mind of all that pain, horror, and revulsion.

I want to remember what I can't and forget what I am destined to remember. I can't do either and probably never will.

POSTSCRIPT

I know that it's hard, if not impossible, for most people to project themselves into the situation we faced, the escalating panic, heart-rattling pressure, and sheer fright consuming us as we steadily saw control over our fate slipping away.

From our perspective, the prisoner, in his condition, posed a real threat to our lives.

There was another ugly truth. As hard as it is to accept for many, and I counted myself among them before I went to Vietnam, war reconfigures the moral compass, at least temporarily. When it comes to life-or-death decisions, war can transform its participants into animal persona, elevating the survival instinct to the highest of priorities.

Yes, our patrol team played God that day, assuming omniscient authority to determine life and death. Maybe others might have acted differently. We'll never know.

I do know this, however. But for the decision to end the life of that prisoner, I and the rest of the patrol team likely wouldn't have survived. I wouldn't be telling the story of what happened now. I wouldn't have had the life I have had.

I don't have guilt about what happened. Instead, I carry with me each day a deep pain from what the war did to me and what it, for a brief, relative time, made me become, stealing part of my humanity in the process. I don't ask for empathy or sympathy. I only hope people can understand at some level what it was like for us in that godforsaken place.

12

WORTHY ADVERSARIES

> I have found the missing link between the higher ape and civilized man; it is we.
> — Konrad Lorenz

"**W**hatever you do, don't fuck with the Rock Apes."

Those were the parting words of smirking, warrior-looking "gunny" Sgt. Bill Robinson at Camp Pendleton. The comment burst out of the blue, like a mischievous afterthought, as we readied to go to war. Sgt. Robinson didn't embellish or explain what he meant. He gave no advice on how to handle such a creature. He tossed the comment into the air, waved, and walked away, chuckling to himself, "Good luck, men."

The impishness with which he made the comment suggested he was messing with us, toying with our anxiety, as if we didn't have enough to worry about. We were going to war. We knew fun times weren't ahead. We knew we might become easy targets. And we knew that grizzled Vietnam veterans like the gunny sergeant had a habit of razzing new guys. It was a privilege they'd earned and delighted in exploiting. It was expected. Shit flowed downhill in the corps.

Still, you had to wonder. Could Rock Apes exist? What were they anyway? How were we to deal with them? Were they an endangered species? Make believe? Yes, that was it, they were a figment of imagination. Besides, they were too weird to think about. We faced more weighty matters.

By the time we had several recon missions under our belts, we had long forgotten the departing remark of Sgt. Robinson. No one, it seemed, gave it a second thought, and nothing we had seen or heard in-country gave us pause to reflect on his words. He was pulling our leg, right? Wrong. He wasn't.

We were on patrol, approaching the end of our day, looking forward to settling down at the night harbor site. The entire day nothing unusual had come to our attention. We'd heard the same noises we knew well, and we sniffed the same odors we expected in our jungle lives. That day, it was business as usual, as much as anything can be considered usual in the jungle.

But as twilight edged and accumulated, fatigue took hold. Unfamiliar noises filtered our way, sounds not covered in the military playbook, sounds we couldn't easily categorize. We did what we were trained to do. We halted on a dime and listened carefully. It sounded like wild thrashing, like someone enthusiastically hacking away at thick vines and elephant grass with a machete, trying to create a clearer path.

At first, we couldn't eliminate the possibility of danger. But it felt different, almost beckoning, inviting us closer. We were disinclined to reverse course and unable to restrain our curiosity, instincts that could place us quickly between a rock and hard place. But we had to find what was out there. We eased down the trail slowly with great care, weapons at the ready, prepared for engagement.

The closer we got, the more erratic the noise. At one point, we stopped and looked at each other in bewilderment. What could it be? We shrugged. Heart tempos increased.

As we got closer to the sounds, we became increasingly sure that whatever we were hearing wasn't the enemy. The sounds were too undisciplined, too nonstrategic. And then, as we approached a narrow clearing in our path, we saw what it was.

Wow.

In plain view was a creature no one had ever laid eyes on, whether in person, on TV, or in a zoo, museum, or magazine. It seemed part baboon, part gorilla, and part human, like a prehistoric humanoid. It stood between four and five feet tall, with an oblong head disproportionate in size to the rest of its body. It was all black with thin bristled hair covering every part of its body, except the face, hands, knees, and presumably the bottom of the feet. Its arms, which hung down to its knees, were thickly muscled, like a weightlifter's, and ended in elongated fingers. It had broad shoulders and a barrel chest. Its feet were wider than a human's and larger than those of a gorilla. It was a strange-looking creature—and it was intimidating.

It paid no attention to us. It continued to slam wildly at the trees and ferociously tear up the jungle, howling from deep within, as if anguished, like it had lost its mind or was suffering the pangs of a romantic heartbreak or a missing family member. It didn't seem like a ritual, more like a cathartic outpouring. We had no way to know, of course, but whatever was going on inside that creature didn't concern us. It was flailing away, paying us no mind. Its physical power was scary.

We stood fixated in place taking in this bizarre spectacle, making sure we remained still and quiet. We were content to play the bystander and watch the creature do its thing. We dared not do anything else. When the creature stopped its craziness, it became perfectly still, catching its breath and meditating in the moment. It apparently had gotten whatever it was out of its system and was ready to move on. It seemed to take a long, deep breath and exhaled, like a runner after finishing a long competitive run. Then, without any fanfare or recognition of us, it slunk into the jungle, barely making a sound, and was gone.

A few days later, after returning to base camp, we reported what we saw. The response was raucous hilarity. Once the laughter died down, we were told we'd had our first exposure to the legendary Rock Ape. Sgt. Robinson at Pendleton had spoken the truth.

We learned that Rock Apes, sometimes referred to as *batutut* or *Nguòi rùng*, were indigenous to Vietnam and possibly neighboring nations. As this one did with us, they normally exit their caves to roam the wild at dusk or after nightfall. They tend to travel in packs, which didn't explain the lone creature we'd stumbled upon. They were aggressive and protective of their kind, and we would be smart not to engage them. They didn't tolerate invaders on their turf and, if threatened, could be dangerous. We added the Rock Ape to our watchlist.

Still, our exposure to the Rock Ape seemed more surreal than real, one of those tales that morphs into myth as people recount the event over time. It was a once-in-a-lifetime experience that got recorded in letters home. But who would believe us? They'd probably think we'd gone jungle mad. Over time, as dangerous and vital patrols demanded our attention and consumed our lives, the experience faded, becoming distant background, another day in the crazy life of a combat soldier in the jungle.

We were about to learn more.

Several weeks later, while plowing through thick elephant grass on a recon mission, with dusk making its way toward us, we heard something behind us. We stopped and listened intently. It appeared that we had stumbled upon enemy troops. We adjusted our position to set up an ambush in the precious time we had. With nerves frayed and excitement in the air, we were poised to go at it in a big way with an unsuspecting enemy. We were jacked up.

Seconds later, a form rose from the bush. We were stunned. It was a Rock Ape ambling in our direction, smack into our kill zone. It stood about four feet and looked half human. We held fire to see what it might do once it got a good look at us. But someone in the unit couldn't contain himself, and the idiot threw a rock at the imposing creature, missing it by less than a foot. The primate dropped his chin and cast us a look as if to say "Really?" It then bent over, picked up several rocks with both hands—damn, its hands were big—and began to return the volley with gusto, pummeling our position with an array of what seemed like small boulders. Its throwing technique left much to be desired, but the velocity and power of its throws were extraordinary. We were under attack, literally, and we had to figure out what to do quickly.

Initially, we couldn't decide whether to laugh or run. As the ape bombarded us, it emitted these ear-piercing, screeching noises, like it was practicing a tribal war cry. It was carrying on much like the first Rock Ape we had stumbled upon, only this time its energy was directed at us, louder and worse, for we had become its enemy. The attack was relentless. Getting smashed with a rock wasn't the only risk. Given where we happened to be, the commotion could give away our position to nearby enemy troops. We had to stop the noise. We had no choice. We had to kill it. While shot rounds would send up a possible red alert, it would be quick and short. So, we fired a few rounds and put the thing down, hoping we hadn't made ourselves too obvious to the other side. We continued on to our nighttime resting position.

We arrived at the harbor site about seven. We were exhausted. We set up our perimeter and kicked back for some well-needed rest. Before we were able to set up an observation post, we heard noises in the brush that got louder with each second. Something was approaching. I was scared shitless and grabbed my weapon.

Before we could figure out what was going on, it began to rain rocks. Conceivably from everywhere. From all sorts of angles. We were under attack—by a pack of Rock Apes!

On instinct, we hunkered down behind tree cover. We knew it wasn't wise to defend ourselves with weaponry, a move that would advertise our position. We had no choice. We had to dodge the missiles and hope the little army of excited primates would eventually tire of throwing rocks. Rocks, tree stumps, chunks of mud, and presumably whatever they could lay their hands on pinged the earth and hit equipment. It was an all-out assault. Oddly, though, they kept their distance. Considering our cowering stance, you'd think they'd try to swarm us. But they stood their ground and pelted us with abandon from an unchanging distance.

It was clear. They had hunted us down to gain a measure of revenge for killing one of their own a few hours earlier. Talk about surreal.

They finally ended their assault in unison, as if signaled telepathically. They got spooky quiet and stared at us. We didn't move and returned the look. They were sending us subliminal messages: *Be forewarned. Don't mess with us. You are getting off lightly.* After several seconds of the quiet standoff, one of them, the largest of the group and apparent leader, took a long look at us, turned, and began to walk away. The rest dutifully followed, and in seconds they were gone.

We suffered no casualties except our dinged pride. During that recon mission, the Rock Apes gave us more trouble than the enemy did. We had a whopper of a story to tell not only fellow Marines at base camp but families and friends back home. If someone had spun a yarn like this to me, without knowing what I know, I wouldn't have believed it.

The Rock Apes had something going for them. When they got mad, they threw rocks, which, while not harmless, seemed a relatively civilized way of resolving differences out in the jungle, certainly superior to using automatic weapons, booby traps, artillery, and defoliant chemicals. We were wise to play pacifist.

It could have gotten ugly. We later learned about other Marines who had engaged a regiment of Rock Apes in battle, and, while no Marine died, many suffered wounds from flung rocks, and numerous Rock Apes died. By comparison, our standoff was peaceful.

Odd as it might sound, I came away with considerable respect for this strange primate. It tracked us down to avenge the death of one of its own, precisely what any Marine unit would do for one of its brothers. That alone deserved admiration and respect. More, unlike what we'd do, it didn't attempt to destroy us. It could have gone at us directly, overrun us, and gone all out in battle. We would have gotten the better of any skirmish like that—we had the firepower—but we wouldn't have emerged unscathed, and many of them would likely have perished. From their standpoint, they showed us mercy and made a point the right way. They didn't ask for much. They wanted to be left alone, to live without interference, in their own house. We were forewarned. We might not get off so easily the next time.

They took the higher road, showed a superior moral code. They demonstrated they could be smarter than we were. Our hats were off to them, until next time.

A felled rock ape, Vietnam.

13

A CLASH IN THE WILD

> But his soul was mad. Being alone in
> the wilderness, it had looked within itself and,
> by heavens I tell you, it had gone mad.
> — Joseph Conrad

D espite the constant craziness, recon patrols sometimes got to enjoy the peacefulness of their surroundings amid the natural sounds and movements of the jungle. The tropical rhythms could be meditative, a soothing reprieve from the sheer madness of war and a temporary buffer against fear and worry. They could bring a return to what was once normal and taken for granted—a brief taste of core humanity.

But what was heard, seen, and felt in the jungle during those cherished interludes inevitably got reduced to military data, morsels needed for protection. We had to learn to distinguish between natural sounds and those that revealed danger. We had to know when wind or harmless scurrying creatures moved the thick bush, elephant grass, or tree leaves or branches, and when the movement meant approaching enemy troops or a lurking sniper. Sometimes detection came easy, like the natural sounds of insects, birds, or monkeys going about their daily routines. Other times, they were less easy to decipher, forming blurs in the mind, especially at night when visibility was virtually nil and nerves more prone to get rattled. The jungle could deceive.

It generally wasn't wise to engage in prolonged internal debate about what was out there. Deliberate speed mattered. You heard what you heard and saw what you saw and allowed your instincts to be the great arbiter, often essential to improving the odds of survival. When life laid so immediately in the balance, as it often did, the smart money erred on the side of assuming imminent danger, mandating instant protective action. It was life reduced to a raw bottom-line equation: kill or be killed. Better to be wrong than dead.

Our patrol leader, Sgt. Mike Larkins, First Recon, Echo Company, found himself in such a predicament one morning at the end of a recon patrol. The recon unit had completed a four-day mission and was gearing up to return to base camp for well-deserved rest before getting hauled back into the bush for the next mission. After being in the bush for several days, recon unit members tended to approach the coming breaks in the action with eager anticipation.

As they wound down from the mission, the unit came across a bomb crater Larkins thought could be an effective LZ for getting extracted to base camp. Because of its depth and breadth and virtual lack of vegetation, the crater could give any chopper wide berth, allowing its rotor blades to move freely. It was, to his way of thinking, an ideally suited spot to land the big bird.

The makeshift landing zone had something else of note. It had a trail running through its center, connecting elephant grass and jungle terrain on both sides. The trail was relatively fresh and wide, and Larkins thought it might be a favorite of local creatures, perhaps even elephants, for moving to and from, or perhaps a route for farmers carrying rice. He also wondered whether the VC kept the path under surveillance. It was possible. He made a mental note.

Before shut-eye that night, with extraction to base camp the sole item on the morning agenda, Larkins kicked back to relax, sharing stories from home with his primary radioman. Both hailed from Ohio, a connection that bonded them. Together, removed from current time and place for a short while, they regaled in recounting lore about Buckeye country. At some point, with the conversation in whispers for protective reasons, they turned to the subject of hunting. The radioman asked Larkins, "What was the largest animal you ever killed." Larkins laughed softly and said, "Well hell, probably the neighbor's dog. I don't know." In truth, Larkins hadn't done much hunting, at least nothing noteworthy, much less killed a deer or anything of that magnitude. The radioman responded, "Larkins you ain't shit unless you kill a tiger." They both laughed and prepared for what sleep they could get under the canopy of the jungle sky.

The next morning, Larkins noticed right off that his men seemed agitated and noisier than normal, behavior that troubled him. He had no interest in attracting hostile forces to their whereabouts, certainly not in the current circumstances. They were on the cusp of getting removed from the fray. To make matters worse, uncharacteristically, his admonitions to keep the noise down drew less than a satisfactory response. The loud banter kept up. Most likely, he figured, his men were overly eager to return to base camp. It had been a grueling four days in the bush, and they understandably were pumped about returning. But whatever the source of the heightened and undisciplined energy, the raised decibels made him nervous despite the presumed relative safety of the location.

As his men prepared for the arrival of the chopper, Larkins went down the trail that led to the landing zone from the south to keep an eye on things, the noise of his men clamoring in the background. He sat in the grass, knees up, and assumed a sentry post. The tall elephant grass towered over him, shielding him from the morning sun, which despite the early hour had become intense. He riveted his eyes down the path of the trail and waited, hopefully for nothing at all except the passage of time. The longer he waited, though, the more he feared his unit might attract the wrong kind of attention. He knew, despite the proximity of the extraction chopper, things could go sideways quickly. Tension gathered in his gut.

He rested his rifle on his knees and continued to watch the trail. Every now and then, he scanned the breadth of the larger area, taking note of his own rising eagerness for the arrival of the big bird. A sense of foreboding began to develop. Then, he thought he saw the elephant grass move in the distance. There was no wind, so the movement got his attention. He thought perhaps he'd imagined it, a distinct possibility. It wouldn't be the first time. But then he was sure he saw movement again. He wasn't imagining.

Larkins stilled himself, focusing on his breathing, trying to get quiet inside and out. He began to think that his greatest fear was about to be realized, that VC troops had heard his men messing around and were slinking their way toward them, braced to toss charges, launch an attack, and try to overrun their position. He rose slightly in the tall grass and gave his men the alert signal, but to his dismay, no one acknowledged it or paid it any mind. He dared not call out. He was in this himself for the time being. He braced.

The weeds got still. Again, he thought, maybe he imagined the earlier movements. But then the thick weeds moved again, this time closer to Larkins and in his direction, less than forty feet away. Not a coincidence, he thought. Something was out there. He eased his right hand down the barrel of his M16, placing it securely on the grip of the weapon with one finger resting easy on the trigger. With the other hand, he quietly and gingerly flicked off the safety latch. He zeroed in on the spot where he last saw the grass flicker. He was ready.

Then, to his astonishment, a lone figure emerged from deep within the elephant grass. It was not a VC or the NVA. It was not a local farmer or rambling South Vietnamese citizen. It wasn't human at all. It was a tiger, moving with silky ease, as if on air, gliding its body through the grass, the tall stems parting like the biblical Red Sea, revealing its massive head and wide eyes. Larkins could see the tiger looking right at him, and it seemed to take measure of the Marine, now standing, alone and directly in front of it down the trail. Their eyes locked. Larkins knew what he was facing. He'd seen Tarzan movies. He'd been to the zoo. He knew what a tiger looked like. This wasn't fantasy. But never for a moment had he imagined ever seeing one up close with nothing to restrain the animal—and within striking distance. The two strangers stared at each other for what seemed a long time, but which lasted probably mere seconds.

Larkins didn't assume the tiger would charge him or that he should try to take him down regardless. He had no base instinct to kill the animal, no natural identity as a hunter. The prospects of a trophy moment didn't zip through his mind. Nor did he know the tiger species in Vietnam was on the road to extinction. The singular consideration for him was whether he was in danger. Unknown to Larkins, while stories existed about tigers attempting to drag Marines away at night, they were scavengers, wary of humans, and habitually fed off old kills. It was rare for a tiger to go after a living human, other than in self-defense or in protection of cubs. Still, one could never be sure of such things. Word had circulated recently that a tiger had mauled and killed a Marine reconnaissance patrol leader in an area close by. Was this tiger stalking and feeding off Marines? Whether this was the same tiger or not, who could say or ever know?

Regardless, Larkin didn't have any of that information at this moment and, equally important, it likely wouldn't have mattered if he did. Even if he were schooled in the world of the Vietnam tiger, he wouldn't have been inclined to calculate the odds of risk and what likely awaited him in this standoff. A tiger in the Vietnam jungle was staring intently at him, and that, no matter how it was sized up, wasn't a good thing. Far from it. His life was at risk. He could be dead in seconds.

Larkins remained in a defensive posture. He kept his eyes fixed on the eyes of the magnificent beast in full display before him. He knew enough not to show fear. He knew to show resolve. He aimed to show the tiger he wasn't going anywhere, wasn't retreating no matter what. The tiger seemed to be thinking the same thing as it stood pat.

Then the tiger blinked and took another step, a single paw outward, not necessarily toward Larkins, but slightly forward as if tiptoeing on the jungle floor, not wanting to disturb anything. Perhaps it was testing the steely, focused Marine, daring him, calling his bluff.

When the tiger took that one careful step, harmless as it may have seemed, whatever its true intent, it was the wrong direction so far as Larkins was concerned. No time now to play around. He discharged his weapon, unloading the entire magazine of twenty rounds in a rapid barrage of fire, hitting the target fourteen times. The tiger went down, face first, with an earth-shattering thud. Remarkably, the tiger tried to rise, tearing up the earth and roaring as if possessed, giving off a scary and maddening death rattle. Taken aback by the power and resilience of the animal, Larkins loaded another magazine into his M16. He then grabbed a grenade and pulled the pin. The tiger got still. It had been unable to rise and now was nestled flat on the ground within the tall elephant grass. Hearing no more sounds from the felled cat and seeing it move no further, Larkins presumed the tiger dead. He reinserted the pin into the grenade and returned it to his magazine pouch. He then walked in the tiger's direction, slowly, keeping his eyes fixed on the prone tiger. When Larkins stood less than five feet away, the tiger seemed to move ever so slightly, a pulsating shake. It then emitted another air-shattering sound, like an explosion of air bursting from deep inside the lungs, a ceremonial exclamation to the call of death. The sound startled Larkins, forcing him to step back instinctively and discharge his weapon again, emptying the second magazine into the downed tiger. With that, it was over.

Sgt. Larkins with his predator

By this time, the recon unit had converged on the scene. Once everyone figured out what had gone down, some panic set in. Everyone knew the commotion Larkins triggered was a loud invitation for hostile attention. The enemy was intimately familiar with the sounds of the M16, as were the Marines with the AK-47 of the enemy. The sounds of two magazines unloading were sure to carry across the distance and be heard. Worse, the chopper hadn't arrived. They had gotten lucky earlier. Five other recon teams were still out in the bush, and somehow headquarters had selected Larkins's unit for extraction first. The question now was whether their luck had run out, as Larkins feared a surge of VC coming at them any minute.

They contacted the helicopter again. The pilot confirmed arrival in three to four minutes and, when hearing of the situation, said he'd try to get there even sooner. The seven Marines had nowhere to go. They had to hang tough and keep fingers crossed. They readied themselves for possible enemy engagement—but each privately hoped luck would prevail again.

Lucky they were. When the chopper began its descent to the LZ, no indication of hostile forces had appeared. After the radioman helped the chopper to the ground, everyone hastily got on board. The process, however, was a little slower than normal, as Larkins insisted they bring an eighth passenger, a dead tiger. Shaking his head in part amusement and part amazement, the pilot didn't resist. What the hell, he thought, why not transport a tiger from the wild to base camp. He had seen enough to know this war had few bounds.

Word of what happened circulated among Marine leadership like wildfire. The powers that be decided to leverage Larkins's jungle feat to bring a form of closure to the family who lost their son a few weeks earlier to a tiger attack. They claimed, without knowing, that the tiger that took the life of the Marine was the same tiger Larkins had vanquished. True or not, the narrative fit. Jungle justice was served, wild-west style.

Sgt. Michael Larkins (left) and Lt. Lou Daugherty display the 300-pound tiger Larkins killed when the animal charged him. The Leathernecks were on a mission 17 miles northwest of Da Nang when they ran into the animal. (USMC)

Unfriendly Tiger Comes Up 2nd Best in Test With Marine

DA NANG, Vietnam (Special) — Six members of E Co., 1st Recon Bn., 1st Marine Div. had been working in an area of Elephant Valley, 17 miles northwest of Da Nang, for four days. Now all that remained of their mission was to wait for the extraction helicopter that would return them to their battalion area.

The Leathernecks had set up a defensive position around the landing zone early in the morning. They scanned the surrounding area for movement and hoped for the quick arrival of the chopper.

Sgt. Michael L. Larkins positioned himself on a trail that led to the landing zone. Suddenly he spotted some movement approximately 150 feet in front of him. He motioned to the Marine beside him to remain quiet and still. Again Larkins detected the movement, but this time he was able to distinguish it. Staring at him through the bushes was the striped face of a 300-pound tiger.

Larkins took aim with his M16 rifle and fired. The bullet caught the animal in the throat and dropped him to the ground. The tiger began to growl and thrash around. Larkins, not wanting to take any chances, shot him again.

Lt. Lou K. Daugherty, the team leader was positioned on the other side of the landing zone when he heard the first shot fired. "I thought we had enemy contact," recalled the lieutenant. Daugherty began making his way in the direction of the fire. Then he and Larkins approached the tiger and discovered it was dead.

Pacific Stars & Stripes
Tuesday, June 9, 1970   7

Daring Save of Recon Team Like 'OK Corral' Revisited

By GUNNERY SGT. JAMES J. OGGERINO
DA NANG, Vietnam (Special) — The wild, wild west, even in its heyday, couldn't match the shootout held recently between the crew of HMM 763's Helicopter Number 8, piloted by 1st Lt. James R. Fuller, and the enemy who were trying to knock ...ming a six-man ...

The helicopter was grimly silent until the ladder was dropped. Then all havoc broke loose. Fire was coming from all directions. The six-man reconnaissance team below was surrounded.

Porteur opened fire first. Then came Belcher's M60 followed almost immediately by Cobb of the left gun and Murray's M79 grenade launcher.

Meanwhile, Fuller was a sitting duck as he kept the helicopter at a steady hover to enable the recon team below to hook on. When the process was complete, Drumwright gave the thumbs-up signal.

All members of the recon team were lifted safely out of the zone and the wounded were delivered to 1st Medical Bn.

Larkins got to keep the tiger. He had the 300-pound animal prepared and treated by a taxidermist in Saigon and shipped to the States. To this day, that tiger remains in his home, a monument to the value of survival instinct and human decisiveness.

14

RUNNING ON EMPTY

> There is magic in misery. Just ask any runner.
> — Ultra Marathoner Dean Karnazes

A shower. A beer. And a bunk bed.

I had never returned from a mission craving those three things more. I didn't care if the shower was cold, the beer warm, or the bunk bed had protruding springs. My wartime standards had pitched super low, not rock bottom, but close enough to see what that might be like.

It had been a planned, seven-day mission that extended into nine grueling days in a sweltering and punishing jungle, the last two days without food. I was plagued with jungle rot and immersion foot, my body a road map of leech invasions, covered with infections. I was depleted, downtrodden, and dirty from a mission that yielded more futility than success and that tested my mettle more than reconnaissance had ever done. I was alive, and for that I was grateful. But I was exhausted to the bone.

I craved the quiet of privacy, a prolonged break from madness. Hell, I wanted more than a long break. I wanted a one-way ticket to far away.

I dragged my tired ass across the tarmac to my hooch and on the way grabbed a beer. Not sure I'd even stay awake long enough to shower, I sat down on my bunk, hanging my legs over the edge, slumped my shoulders, and with a numb mind began to wash warm beer down my dusty throat. A minute or two later, my beer half empty, the door to the hooch swung open, and our patrol leader, Lt. Lou Daugherty, entered, announcing he had something "important" to discuss. That was the last thing I wanted to hear. What came next blew me away.

He said word around Camp Reasoner was that I had talent as a distance runner and had enjoyed success back home running competitively. I didn't deny it. Most everyone knew that before I arrived at Camp Reasoner, Sgt. Michael Larkins had ruled the roost of all runners in the camp until given the chance, I raced and beat him. Larkins was shocked, and to this day, fifty years later, proudly remembers the frustration of the lost race. So, yes, I had a deserved reputation around the compound for running long distances. What of it?

Daugherty said that senior leadership had organized an event to pit soldiers from Australia, South Korea, Vietnam, and the U.S. against each other to compete in several track and field events, a makeshift mini-Olympics. He wanted to know if I'd be willing to run as a representative of our battalion.

I was of two minds. One was, no way. The last thing I needed was extracurricular physical activity. The other part, truer to my core, found the invitation tantalizing. If I could summon the energy, I might relish flashing back to my scholastic, high school, and college days as a long-distance runner.

I took another swig of warm beer and said, "I'll think about it."

"You do that," he said, in a way that left no doubt what he expected me to do. He turned and left. I drained the beer, got prone on my bunk, and fell asleep. No shower that night.

While I pondered the "invitation," word circulated around Camp Reasoner—I cannot imagine how, Lt. Daugherty—that I had committed to run for the battalion.

My background in distance running at Novato High School and the College of Marin in Marin County included the 5,000-meter run, which is where they wanted to enter me. The more I thought about it, the more I warmed to the idea. I hadn't forgotten the sweet taste of competitive running juices, and I could use a few swigs. I told Lt. Daugherty I'd represent the battalion.

Event organizers had imposed a qualification round, akin to Olympic trials. To qualify for the medal round, I had to finish among the top twenty-five out of sixty runners. The trials were around the corner, leaving me little time to get ready. I had to rely on rusty skills that had been languishing in storage for two years.

I placed twenty-fifth, latching on to the last spot, barely qualifying for the medal round. Daugherty was none too pleased.

"I thought you were better than that, Walton. I'd hate for you to embarrass the whole damn battalion. Maybe you should give it up."

He had a point. I didn't look good. But in fairness, I had no time to train. His caustic comments struck a nerve.

"How about this?" I said. "If I place in the final, whether first, second, or third, you know, if I medal, I get R and R in Hawaii." I smiled ear to ear.

Daugherty laughed heartily. "You want me to get you to Hawaii?"

"If I place, if I medal." More serious this time.

I had asked a lot. R and R in Hawaii was generally restricted to officers or married or engaged Marines. I was none of them.

He yanked his head back with a look that suggested he thought I'd gone mad, but then he smiled.

"Well, Walton, I'll let people know you'll be gone for a short while. You worry about medaling."

What did that mean? It didn't take me long to figure out. We did not have a deal as such. He knew what I had to do and had, implicitly, agreed to turn the other cheek. Somewhere, somehow, he would protect my absence. But I never found out what, if anything, he did. Two things I did know: the good lieutenant wouldn't rat me out—if things went okay—and if the shit hit the fan, the conversation we had never happened or never happened the way it did happen.

He offered me his hand, and I shook it, a handshake in the spirit of "good luck, soldier."

I was on my own and had to figure out how to get officer dress greens and military orders that allowed me to take R & R in Hawaii. Lt. Daugherty was out of the picture. And other than him, I had beaucoup connections at the time. My only viable solution as I could tell was to grease the palms of office personnel to give me what I needed. Those underpaid and underappreciated folks might like the smell and feel of some negotiable greenbacks, real American dollars, which in Vietnam were considered contraband and hard to come by.

Insane, I know. I risked a court martial and time in military prison and, of course, a dishonorable discharge. The truth was, however, as crazy as it may sound to the casual observer, I didn't care. I truly didn't. The alternative was more time in the oppressive, triple-canopy jungle where the odds of surviving were long. Jail would have sucked big time. But I would have remained a breathing organism.

I went for it.

I first approached someone in the supply depot to provide me an officer's uniform bearing the nameplate, "Lt. Darren Walton." I don't recall whom I persuaded or how much money I put on the table—except I know it was major bucks and put a serious dent in my meager cash flow—but it worked. In short order, I received well-fitting Marine dress greens.

Next, I went to the admin building. There, I cajoled the clerk to prepare orders allowing "Lt. Darren Walton to take 'R & R in

Hawaii'" during a specified time. Again, I have no clue whom I charmed or how much dinero I put in his palm—again major bucks—but it did the trick.

Did Lt. Daugherty set any of that up behind the scenes? Did he use some wink-wink coded language to help me out? Possibly, but I doubt it. He was clear on how he intended to handle things. Still, stranger things have happened in the armed forces.

Once I had the orders, I stayed under the radar, keeping to myself, trying not to mix with anyone—all my best efforts at being invisible.

I also made romantic arrangements. I got in touch with Jane stateside, who lived in Marin County and was my high school sweetheart. I asked her to meet me in Hawaii during the R & R. She was game, and I was getting eager to enjoy the trip.

* * *

I now had ample motivation to stoke my natural competitive nature and pride. Still, I had my work cut out for me. I didn't know the competition, except I knew that twenty-four runners dusted me the first time, and to stand a chance at medaling, I'd have to perform considerably better than I'd managed in the trials, moving from twenty-fifth to the top three, not to put too fine a point on it.

I learned after the fact that the first-place finisher in the trials was Dennis Leaf, a Marine officer. Like me, Leaf got recruited to represent his unit and, in turn, drafted his running buddy, R. C. Miller, another Marine officer. Miller qualified as well, placing second or third in the trials. Both were accomplished runners who ran track and field and cross country in high school and college. They also ran most nights in Vietnam around a short track in their compound. I was glad not to know all that before the race, except I would have loved to know that my best competition was two Marine officers, a morsel of reconnaissance that would have fanned my existing competitive flames.

In the few days between the trial and the final, I trained as best I could. Running at the Camp Reasoner compound catapulted me back to my school running days. I recalled specific races and what it felt like to run as part of a team. I remembered the thrill of victory and reminisced about running on the hilly, uneven trails in Marin County and the joy it gave me. I had an uplifting sense of déjà vu.

The night before the race I did not sleep well, tossing and turning all night. I was nervous, not so much about the R & R deal that hung in the balance of my performance but of competing and not doing well. My pride fueled my emotional anticipation. The good news was that for some reason, which I cannot recall, my mother had sent me my running shoes. A nice, serendipitous touch, I thought.

The next morning, I took a cold shower to get my mind straight, had breakfast, and awaited my chauffeured ride to Da Nang for the race, set for the early afternoon. The scene on arrival was something to behold. We were to run inside a soccer stadium on a dirty, rocky, and uneven track, which fifty years later R. C. Miller described looked as if someone "had scraped it off with a road grader that was missing forks."

And, to top it off, it was ninety degrees and ninety percent humidity, hardly ideal for a long-distance competition.

The spectators, numbering about one thousand, assembled inside the track while scores of athletes from South Korea, Vietnam, Australia, and the U.S. milled around. As races unfolded, local children enthusiastically cheered their favorites while older kids rode bikes to keep pace with runners inside the track. It was quite the scene.

Despite the presence of so many people, I felt isolated. My recon team could not attend to cheer me on. I wanted them there, but the powers that be sent them on a new mission without me. There was, after all, a war going on. I worried about them and felt bad I couldn't discharge my responsibilities as patrol point man.

Before too long, the time had come for the 5,000-meter competition, and the twenty-five of us got summoned. I quickly scanned the group, trying to size them up, but that was more habit than useful. I went inside myself, my mind wandering again to prior races in the U.S. with high school buddies—many of whom were All-American or high school Hall of Fame runners. Nostalgia set in. I wished my school days running buddies could be there with me and run alongside. How much fun, I thought, it would be for us to join forces one more time.

As my mind strayed, I realized I was again getting nervous and feeling isolated. How did I wind up in this godforsaken place!? Running a race in the middle of a jungle war! I had not run competitively in two years. How was I supposed to do this with only one week to recover from the last debilitating mission, not to mention, virtually no preparation? What kind of shape was I in? Was I going to fail?

I emptied my mind again, and as if on a pilgrimage, my breathing soft, I walked in deliberate steps to the area near the starting line. With each step I felt the rising temperature, a steady drumbeat of thick heat. The sun would soon be overhead and brutal. My heart beat a little faster as I pondered the sheer magnitude of the athletic test that awaited me. I scanned the competition, a pageantry of multi-hooded and -colored sweatsuits from different countries and our own different militaries. Most everyone had their eyes down. What were they thinking? Were they thinking at all? I looked beyond the readying runners toward the crowd and absorbed the soft buzz of chatter emanating from the assembled spectators.

A loudspeaker directing the runners to the starting line interrupted my trance-like focus. The moment had arrived. Adrenaline shot through my body from my legs to my heart. I took a deep breath and slowly exhaled. I was still nervous. Maybe that was a good thing. Maybe it meant I was ready.

I gingerly placed my right big toe inches behind the starting line and with the ball of my foot, felt the ground. I dug in a little. I exhaled again.

I tried to empty my mind again, free myself of nerves and insecurities. It didn't work. Some runners shook their hands and arms back and forth to release energy and settle themselves. Others jumped up and down like pogo sticks, trying to get blood flowing. Still others stood tall and moved a few paces behind, preferring to start behind the pack. Everyone had a ritual.

In their own way, most everyone was skittish. Everyone looked ahead now. No eyes were down anymore.

The loudspeaker broke the silence again.

"Gentlemen . . . take your marks, get set," and *crack*!

May 1, 1970   SEA TIGER

Vietnamese Capture Sports Festival As Thousands Cheer

Americans, Koreans and Vietnamese runners bolt from the starting point of the 5,000 meter run.

The start of the race, Dennis Leaf far left, me far right

The starting gun washed away the jittery stillness around us, and the crowd roared its excited approval. People rushed forth like a herd of buffalo stampeding in the heat, different forms of breathing, random grunting, hearts throbbing, dust flying, legs and feet pounding, and elbows flying, as runners jockeyed for position and a comfortable running space.

The race was on, and an all-consuming surge of energy replaced my nervousness. It was a familiar place, and I realized in an instant how much I missed it. I was in my element.

I felt good but wasn't getting anywhere. The ensemble of runners bunched up for the first mile, and then, as often is the case, different groups formed and splintered into a hierarchy of positions, each with an identified leader. After two laps, I slipped quickly to the back. Not good.

Lagging Behind Early in the Race

Trickles of panic filled my gut as I found it hard to keep up with the main section of the pack. Had I lost my mojo? Had I been off running too long? Had I bit off more than I could chew?

As I tortured myself with doubt, I looked up and saw that I'd dropped into last place!

Fear and anxiety overwhelmed me as with a sense of desperation, I tried to keep pace with the caboose pack. I was stunned. What was going on? At home, I competed well with the best. These runners were not better. I knew that implicitly. But I began to doubt myself. I felt premature fatigue. What would my recon team think of me? I couldn't let them down.

I had to find a way. I had to dig deep. I had to block out the environment.

It was a long race, twelve laps. I had ample time to close the gaps, provided my body was up to the task. I began to isolate my sense of being from all else. I redirected myself to a time past and the many races I had logged in cool breezes along the Pacific Ocean and through redwood forests. At home, I habitually ran in the hills and enjoyed the beautiful landscaping for which Marin County is known. It was part of the wonder and thrill of running. The home environment injected instant relaxation, made me part of the surroundings, as nature partnered with me as a runner. Here, however, the environment was an impediment, a distraction, mainly because of all the local kids cheering, chirping, and trying to keep pace with us. I refocused on finding the graceful fluidity of movement I enjoyed at home, that mindless romp through uneven terrain and up and down steep inclines.

My body eased. Adrenaline burned off. My pace smoothed. Autopilot set in.

I looked up to see that the first runners had started to pull away. If they got too far ahead, I'd never close the race competitively. I had to accelerate while keeping calm and methodical. Any anxiety, any sense of panic, would doom me.

No matter how I performed, I knew what was coming: the pain, the kind that makes you think your body is on the cusp of collapse. As a competitive athlete, I dealt with that type of pain often. It isn't fun, but I had learned to manage it. Now, I didn't know if my jungle-reshaped body could overcome the pain that was sure to come.

Like clockwork, the numbing pain came and coursed throughout my body, and once it started, I knew it might never end. I had to will it away.

And then I found a familiar mental space. I became single-minded, pushed out all negative energy, and tapped into the rhythmic trance that clears the mind during a long run, essential for maximum output. I reclaimed my runner warrior spirit, and my confidence grew. I felt lighter. I knew I'd be fine if I stayed positive, kept patient, and didn't lose poise.

I felt in command. I resolved to pick off runners, one at a time, a divide-and-conquer strategy, recording tiny victories in succession. As I progressed, more runners faded. I had reestablished my ground.

I worked my way up. The heat increased, robbing all runners of precious energy, as the temperature climbed to 100 degrees and an equal measure of humidity. My in-country experiences helped. My body knew jungle oppression. I had stood up against repeated heat-infested days. They no longer rattled me.

Making Up Ground

My muscles tightened around my shoulders. My arms got heavier. My lungs burned. My heart pounded. My leg muscles screamed.

Please don't let me die.

One mile left. I closed in on the runners directly in front of me and found myself right behind the lead pack of four runners. I had to improve the odds. They were, hands down, a different caliber of runner than the others left behind. Each of the four, each an American, was fixated on winning. This could get interesting.

I started to taste the possibility of victory. I knew I could beat those guys. I was getting stronger. My lungs continued to burn. My muscles screamed and my heart soared. I was all in. The crowd didn't exist. Nothing existed except my purpose. I was in my private space, and it felt super good.

My vision blurred and my ears rang. For the first time, I strained for oxygen and had difficulty breathing.

Half a mile to go. I jumped past two of the runners and squeezed into third place. I knew in that moment I would medal. The only question was, could I grab the gold? Winning the whole damn thing was all that mattered. I didn't focus on Hawaii or anything else. I was dialed into the gold medal.

The sound of feet pounding the turf had changed. The two men in front of me were gliding over the top of the track. They were pros.

Quarter mile to go.

I passed the second position and pulled within one long stride of the leader. I'd later learn it was Dennis Leaf, who had won the trials. Blond haired and good looking, the guy had a gait like a human gazelle. He glanced over his right shoulder and smiled at me. The guy smiled! Like he was out for a casual stroll. He was having fun while I was in a life-and-death struggle to win.

It was him and me keeping pace with each other. I can win, I told myself. A fog of exhaustion swept over me. I opened the throttle. My lungs were on fire. I could feel my heart bouncing off my chest cavity.

We had 100 yards left.

I tried to push him to the outside lane. Leaf knew I was up to the challenge and inched to the side making it harder to pass, effectively blocking me. It was a deft, effortless move. I was dealing with a special talent. I was impressed.

I backed off slightly to save energy for the final push. I wasn't confident I could get ahead of him until the end. But I felt down the stretch that I could sprint by him. My final strategy locked in, I tucked comfortably behind him. I figured I'd post him on the straightway and try to blow past him. I knew my only chance was to out "kick" him.

I put it all on the line. I maximized my output. Leaf stayed steady and strong. He was coasting. He knew my plan. He had me under control.

And then, he flew ahead, like getting shot out of a cannon, outkicking me like no one had ever done before, and with ease, as if he could keep running all the way to Cambodia. He was gone, and I could do nothing about it. He left me in awe.

Second place and the silver medal.

Silver is not gold.

So sad.

How did I lose after so much effort? What could I have done better? Something? Nothing? Did it matter?

I should have been proud and ecstatic. I was, instead, demoralized. Sure, I medaled, garnering the silver, but I didn't win. As a runner, I had to win. To make matters worse, right after the race, I learned that Leaf was an officer, which deepened the pain of loss. I hated losing to an officer. The saving grace was that he was a Marine. That counted for something.

We shook hands and took pictures. Leaf didn't stick around. He beat me and went to his hooch. Later, according to firsthand accounts, he commented to his unit that he won a medal, and well, that was it. He moved on, while I never forgot, tormented by the loss, which has stayed with me all these years.

Congratulating Leaf (reluctantly)

When I decided to write this book, I had to find Leaf. My co-author and I began the search. We learned that Leaf passed in 2015. We tracked down his wife, Anna, who was gracious in talking to us and providing information about her late husband. She also introduced us to some of his friends, including R. C. Miller. Despite placing in the top three in the trials, Miller finished last that day, not for lack of skill, but because the poor man had the flu. He ran to support Leaf.

Leaf grew up on a farm in Rockford, Illinois, where he first tried his hand at running. Like most runners do, he ran initially for solitude and to create distance from life's stresses. He turned out to be a natural, and his friends encouraged him to run competitively. One friend fondly referred to him as "half deer."

Leaf was a cross-country star at Fort Atkinson High School in Wisconsin. He later attended Carthage College (class of '67) which, much to his chagrin, did not have a cross-country program when he enrolled. Not a problem. He convinced the Carthage AD to assemble a cross-country team, the first in the school's 117-year history.

He practiced relentlessly, running long distances ninety minutes a day along with repeated sprints up hills and interval speed work on the track. His strengths were a steady, consistent pace, great stride, and boundless endurance. Ironically, he wasn't known for a great finishing kick, although you never would have thought that when he outkicked me. Everyone said he could run forever, never lost steam, and relished being the frontrunner so he could outpace the competition.

After graduating from Carthage, he attended Northwestern Lutheran Theological Seminary. He left the divinity school in 1968, and eventually, feeling the call of duty, enrolled in the Marines.

After Vietnam, he remained a prodigious runner, logging his times each day. He competed in over two hundred races, twenty-four of which were marathons, including the Marine Corps Marathon. Running was his identity.

Leaf was universally loved, an innately gracious and good-hearted person, incessantly cheerful, and respected by all.

A worthy opponent bested me. I am proud to have run against him.

Leaf competed one last time in January 2015, a seven-mile competition he handled, despite being terminally ill. After the race, he announced to family and friends, "I'm done." He succumbed to lung cancer six months later, on June 20, 2015. He was seventy.

* * *

There is more to this story, and it has to do with the R & R trip to Hawaii. As the trip approached, I began to have new thoughts. I had long lost any sense of patriotism for the war, to the extent I had any to speak of from the start. It was not that I felt unpatriotic, but I had grown tired of what increasingly seemed a futile and misguided national military quest. Like so many others similarly situated, my drive became survival. I had more than my fill of the jungle war and began to think about not returning from R and R. The more I thought about it, the more captivating the idea became. I said my goodbyes to my close combat friends, telling them I might not return. We still remember that conversation fifty years later.

When travel day arrived, I made my way from Da Nang to Gaum to Honolulu. Several of us were slated to take a van to the army base, the site of the R & R and a beautiful resort. When the person in charge of transit started checking off names, I receded and didn't respond when he called mine. I decided in that moment to di di mau to San Francisco.

I alerted Jane to the change in plans. I had civilian clothes with me on board. Once I made the decision—effectively to go AWOL—I beelined to a bathroom and changed out of the dress greens. I can't recall what I did with the officer threads. I probably dumped them in a terminal garbage can. I certainly didn't take them with me. I then booked a flight to San Francisco. And so, the van left without me, thinking "Lt. Walton" had missed the flight.

My time in California is vague in my head except for a few things. I recall going to rock concerts to see The Doors, Janis Joplin, and Big Brother and the Holding Company. Most of all, I recall a sit-down discussion with my father. He didn't treat me like a kid. He respected how I approached the situation and appreciated the complexity of the decision I faced.

My father had his own Marine history. He'd fought in WWII in the battle of Okinawa, receiving a Purple Heart. It was his first engagement. His buddy next to him, knowing he was a bit green and untested, admonished him, "Get your head down, you idiot. You're going to get your head shot off." Minutes later, a mortar landed nearby, sending shrapnel into my father's face and kill-ing his buddy. He was, as can be imagined, patriotic, a position sealed when in the bloody battle of Tarawa, he lost his brother, a member of the Carlson Raiders. My unit, First Recon, is a di-rect descendant of the Raiders. My father had the view that the communists were engaged in a domino effort through Indo-china to consolidate their global power. But he also began to see that the U.S. became corrupted and greedy to the point where corporate profit drove the military machinery. For the first time, he acknowledged that the Vietnam War was not the just war he thought it was.

The risks had gotten closer to the hearts of the family. Surpris-ing me, he urged that I consider relocating to Canada. We had family there, and I could be comfortable and supported. After much debate, I announced, "I'm going to Canada."

No sooner had I decided to leave the country and lay down stakes with our North American neighbor, I saw a news segment with famed broadcast journalist Walter Cronkite. Watching the war on TV was itself an eye-opener. But more than that, it trig-gered a powerful sense of loyalty to the men I'd left behind in my reconnaissance unit. How would I feel if I weren't on point on a mission, and something bad happened to them?

I knew then that I couldn't go to Canada. I had to be with them. We were a tight brotherhood. I loved those guys and couldn't abandon them. I had to return to the jungle.

I spent about the same time in California as I would have spent enjoying the R and R program. I don't recall my return journey to Vietnam, except I know I kept mum about what had gone down, and no one asked questions. I was needed in the jungle, and that seemed all that mattered. I was primed to go back to work. And like what often happens in life, it turned out to be a case of "Be careful what you ask for."

— 15 —

"WE'VE BEEN DISCOVERED"

> No hero is mortal till he dies.
>
> — W. H. Auden

Those three words shattered the air against the backdrop of small arms fire pinging the jungle foliage, and amid the chaos, Marines hustled in many directions for cover.

They were words that our recon unit never wanted to hear and the radio operator who barked them never wanted to utter. They meant quite plainly that the enemy had found our small recon unit and had started to rain hell upon us with but one goal in mind: killing us all.

The plaintive plea to base camp—"We've been discovered"— sounded the familiar alarm that the unit was in deep trouble and, like most recon units, ill-equipped for sustained battle and in need of an emergency extraction. It meant, too, that the best laid plans of military intelligence had gone amuck, and that no matter how successful the mission had been up to that point, in the absence of a speedy intervention—military or divine—the mission would tragically fail, meaning several if not all of us were about to cross the Jordan.

While those words sounded desperate, they also conveyed hope, evidence that radio communication was alive and well and that we had a fighting chance. So long as we had radio contact, no matter how insane things got, extraction and thus survival could happen. That is why our units often used two radiomen, improving the odds of survival, which, after all, was the goal of all goals, making it home alive and intact. The radio operators were our lifelines.

It also explained why the first bit of critical training information that newbie radio operators received came in the form of a number: 5. Often, instructors posted that numeral prominently on the white board and challenged the collective souls in training to recognize its significance. The results normally were stares, shrugs, and headshakes.

The digit stood for five seconds, the life expectancy of a radioman in a jungle firefight. As a teaching point, the lesson was manifest: know what you're doing every moment; don't cut corners; stay forever poised; and pay homage to detail. It may well save your life, not to mention the lives of many others. Make no mistake of your vital importance. Never forget, never.

While five seconds might be a slight exaggeration designed to make an important training point, it was close enough to the grim reality that awaited the recon radiomen. A more hopeful barometer may have been thirty seconds. Give or take the seconds, they mattered.

And so, while we scrambled, the radio operator had the urgent task of finding a safe place to operate, relatively speaking. He took his teachings to heart that if the enemy had its way, he would be an early casualty, and we all knew, the enemy included, that without him, we were as good as gone.

It was not easy. Apart from the chaotic danger that swirled about a recon unit embroiled in a firefight, radiomen were magnetic targets. Radio chatter easily pinpointed their location, despite the noise of battle. The same was true of radio volume from incoming communications. The volume dial rested on the back of the radio operator and wasn't always easily accessible. Radio noise was a location giveaway.

Then there was the matter of radio antennae. The shorter version, about three feet, was more manageable and didn't present that great a target, especially when entrenched in jungle vegetation. The problem was that the shorter antenna didn't work as well in the clogged jungle environment, often yielding to the ten-foot version, a virtual bullseye.

The ability to move well, stay focused, and remain keenly attentive was made even more difficult by the sheer weight of the gear radio operators hauled around. All in, which included active and extra batteries and the NESTOR encryption device (KY-38), the PRC-77 radio system could weigh as much as fifty pounds, which was fifty pounds—in addition to combat gear—on the back of the radio operator every step of the way in the unforgiving jungle.

Radio operators were also responsible for calling in airstrikes, increasing their already weighty responsibilities. They had to know the codes like they knew nothing else, which wasn't as easy as it might sound. Codes changed constantly to limit the ability of the enemy to decipher the secret ins and outs of internal military language, which the NVA became adept at doing. And communicating codes amid blazing warfare didn't always come seamlessly. There were many distractions, to put it mildly. It didn't take much of an error to heap friendly fire on a unit embroiled in enemy danger. The margin for error was, at most, exceedingly slim. The same was true for reading maps. It was not like spreading them out on a table at base camp and leisurely dissecting details over a cup of coffee. They had one chance to get it right, or people could die.

These skills were at a premium when it came to emergency extractions. The unit typically had a designated landing zone, a rendezvous spot where they were directed to go at the conclusion of the mission, where the chopper could easily land and retrieve the entire unit without fanfare. Weather could complicate things, forcing an alternative plan, but better that than being under fire and scrambling for an exit location.

But in an emergency, all bets were off. The unit didn't have the luxury of a preplanned location. It had to find a new, relatively safe, and workable location—and pronto. In football terms, the radio operator in conjunction with the patrol leader had to call an audible, no easy task in the Vietnam jungle. Communication was essential. Radio operators knew many pilots by name and were aware as well of their individual idiosyncrasies. In emergency moments, radio operators became the band leader, directing traffic and steering everyone to safety.

Once the emergency extraction location was selected, the radioman had to help the pilot find an opening to drop the forty-to-fifty-foot ladder between the trees, filtering out the intensity around them, yet keeping a sense of the enemy and the increasing risk. Once that was done, he turned to shepherd unit members, one by one, up the extraction ladder, staying in contact with the pilot, while the CH-46 hovered above them. Each second was treasured since the enemy was either in relative proximity or closing in.

That meant, by necessity, radiomen were the last in line up the extraction ladder. They had the means of communication. And the longer the wait to get everyone up, the greater the risk of getting hit and taken down, putting everyone in ultimate peril, and the less likely the big bird would hang around for the radioman to get on the ladder. Pilots were razor tough and had courage to spare, but they weren't stupid and understood well the nuances of danger. They weren't about to risk an entire unit, their copilot, and themselves, or their chopper, if they felt the moment of reckoning was about to arrive.

Consider this actual event.

Our recon unit got discovered, and the radioman called for help: we needed an emergency extraction. The patrol leader and the radioman found a spot, but when the helicopter arrived, it was unable to let down to turf, meaning everyone had to clamp on to the ladder to live. The chopper dropped the ladder amid the triple-canopy trees. The radio operator directed each member of the unit toward and up the ladder while the enemy was in hot pursuit and inching closer. It was a wild scramble. The radioman was last. Meanwhile, the chopper started taking direct fire, and the pilot became increasingly nervous about staying. The big bird was rapidly becoming a sitting duck. And when shots began to ricochet off the side of the chopper, the pilot had had enough and started to lift. The radioman, however, remained. Left with no other choice, he grabbed the next-to-last rung of the rising ladder and threw his legs through the bottom rung without snapping in the ring to secure his position. He wrapped his legs around the bottom rung as securely as he could, but before he could get a more secure position, the upward thrust flipped him backward, and he hung upside down, his legs holding on for dear life. As the chopper continued to lift, he started scraping trees, which ripped his radio, the codes, and his rifle from him. He watched them drop to the ground. He managed to pull himself up with his legs and lock his arms around the next rung, and there he stayed, dangling in the air, not tied in, as the chopper made its way back to base camp. He and the others survived.

* * *

Some Marines aspired to be in communications. Many others, however, got pressed into service to meet the constantly changing needs of war. Often, that meant the most recent Marine assigned to our company got rewarded with a radio—and a three-day training course. Next man up. Duty calls.

The Vietnam War claimed the lives of more than its share of radiomen. It was inherently a hazardous duty and often the stuff of hero making. People are living today because of the competence, dedication, and courage of radio operators. A deep bow to them all.

— 16 —

DI DI MAU

A hero is one who knows how to
hang on one minute longer.
— Novalis (German poet)

A perk of our reconnaissance work was regular breaks between patrols. For me, it was a time to do little, other than relax, read, and write letters. The action breaks were welcome calms before the guaranteed-to-follow unpredictable storms. We knew that once we returned after a patrol, in a matter of days, we'd be sent on a new mission, like night follows day.

After the horrific prisoner snatch experience, I was hoping for a long break. My mind and soul needed repairing. It was not to be.

I was lounging in the hooch, reading a book, when Sgt. Jacobson poked his head inside and said, "We're going out in two days. Briefing is tomorrow. Start getting ready."

His face betrayed the lead. The next mission was another prisoner snatch. Talk about déjà vu all over again.

Jacobson would be the patrol leader, and I'd walk point. I had a bad feeling about this one from before the start.

I was reminded how recon units like ours were often in perilous situations despite our stated purpose. We were to gather intelligence. We were not supposed to get it on with the enemy. For that reason, as noted earlier, we weren't equipped for extended battle. It meant we could travel lighter than grunt units. It also meant we could, in theory at least, move faster. Gather intelligence and return.

Sure, we had weapons. But we were six or seven men deep, and, other than running across an enemy loner or two on a trail, we'd be outnumbered in any skirmish. If we detected a larger unit in our vicinity, we were supposed to call in artillery or other forces, leaving it to others to handle. If we had to fight a unified force, we would be in deep trouble.

We prepared for this new mission with the usual diligence, pouring over the maps and the prior relevant recon reports, identifying the planned insertion and extraction landing zones, getting an early feel for the anticipated terrain, and receiving weather forecasts. We were told without a hint of drama that we would be in a hot zone from the chopper insertion and beyond.

The morning of the patrol we boarded the CH-46, a familiar member of the Purple Fox squadron, again with virtually no words exchanged among the team and chopper crew. Before the cobwebs had cleared in my head, we were on our way. As we climbed the sky, my mind wandered. I began to get homesick. I envisioned all the things I wanted to do after I returned, a wish list of must-dos. I felt a deep longing to be gone from Vietnam. I felt isolated and misplaced, like getting off at the wrong bus stop after a prolonged daydream. I had never had these yearnings before, and they troubled me.

My reminiscence ended abruptly when the descent to the LZ began.

It didn't start out well. The chopper couldn't land. The pilot had found a clearing along a hillside, but once he got close, we could see the ground was flush with a massive mound of elephant grass and bamboo that stood about eight feet. We didn't have a level spot to land.

The pilot lowered the chopper as low as he could and began to hover and lift to stay balanced. He told us we'd have to jump out. We were a good ten feet from the ground in a dangerous zone. The longer we stayed inside, the greater the risk. The pilot was getting antsy. He didn't want to be floating in the air as target practice.

No one said a word. We looked at each other with skepticism, knowing a drop of that length could cause injuries. Then, Jacobson took the leap, hit the ground hard with bended knees and on both feet, toppled to the ground, got up, and flashed a thumbs-up. The pilot shouted, "Now or never, hotshots, I've got to di di mau." He wasn't bullshitting. No one wanted to jump, but we had no choice. One at a time, we jumped off the back, or in some cases, literally fell out, landing hard and rolling into each other and our backpacks.

Our rifleman sustained a bad ankle injury. The corpsman taped the ankle and cleared him to continue. While a hobbling injury, it wasn't so bad to warrant medevacking him. He took it in stride, literally. We hoped he wouldn't slow us down.

We set up the usual body perimeter as the chopper disappeared into the sky. Because we were in a red zone, we stayed low to the ground, everyone on their knees, behind the high grass, waiting for things to get quiet. Except for the patrol leaders consulting the maps over whispers, no one said a word. It was only 9 a.m., and the sun had begun its beat-down assault with a vengeance, robbing us of oxygen before we even got started.

Less than ten minutes later, we were on our way.

The path was the worst of its kind. It was the thickest of the thick of the jungle—muddy, thorny, boulder-ridden, and steep— and our progress was painfully slow. The conditions were ripe for the entire fleet of insects and reptiles. The jungle was not inclined to show us mercy on this patrol. By the end of the first day, I knew we'd be exhausted, our spirits dampened. The heat was brutal and the air wet. The prospect of getting to our destination with little in our tanks were likely.

I led the way. We spaced well between the seven of us, but not so far as to lose sight of anyone. We had a well-trained, professional group. We each knew our roles and how to handle ourselves.

Sgt. Jacobson was behind me. From time to time, I glanced over my shoulder without breaking stride to check in with him. It was dark and dense, even in daylight. But we could get visuals on each other, never uttering a word, always communicating with eye contact, body language, or hand signals. I felt safe with Sgt. Jacobson and comfortable relying on him, which counted for a lot. Still, his presence didn't eliminate the angst I continued to feel about this patrol. I was turning my head to him more than usual.

We battled terrain every step of the way, wait-a-minute vines ripping into our clothes and flesh, mud keeping us from getting any ground traction, thick unbendable bamboo and large boulders blocking our paths, and mosquitos, leeches, and ants tormenting our defenseless selves. Sometimes, I had to break a path for the others because none existed.

By 11 a.m., we had to stop for water. We were dehydrated. I'd been in-country several months, and the past two hours humping the jungle was the worst I'd ever experienced, slipping and sliding the whole time. I could have easily downed my entire water supply in one sitting. Sgt. Jacobson earlier warned us about drinking too much. He knew what we faced. He repeated the admonition. We hadn't gotten farther than a couple of hundred yards. We would need water in the days ahead like never before. We needed to exercise discipline.

We resumed the journey. At one point, I couldn't see well enough ahead to continue with safe assurance. I thrust my hand in the air to stop the train of Marines behind me. I gave Sgt. Jacobson a signal to convey that I intended to climb a nearby tree to get a longer view. I climbed about ten to fifteen feet up and scanned the area. What I saw reflected what we had learned in our briefing and from the maps. We had a good azimuth, a working line toward our destination. I got down, gave Sgt. Jacobson a thumbs up, and back to humping we went.

Sgt. Jacobson called it a day earlier than planned. It was coming on 4:30 p.m. We normally went to about 6 p.m. He knew the whole lot of us were exhausted. He got no argument from me. It had been the toughest single day on patrol in my experience. We found a strategic hillside above the trail to camp and to get some well-needed rest for the night. Tomorrow would be a big day.

We put Claymores around for a perimeter, assigned the two-hour radio watches, and confirmed asshole buddies for the morning.

After that, it became quiet. We were too tired to do anything other than ease into the night. Besides, like always, we had to be super careful not to betray our position. Everyone pretty much was left to their own thoughts and below-the-radar activities.

I tried to relax by reading before light vanished. I had brought a book I started at Camp Reasoner, *Stranger in a Strange Land*, Robert Heinlein's work of science fiction about the journey of a human who comes to Earth after being born on Mars and raised by Martians. The book seemed eerily apt in the circumstances.

I picked up the book and read myself into drowsiness. I arranged my poncho liner as a blanket and laid down and had no difficulty sleeping. I got a solid four to five hours, until being awoken for my assigned two-hour radio watch.

In the world of the combat soldier, radio watches are their own species of war experience. For two hours, in utter darkness, sitting still as a rock, you are on constant high alert, listening and observing. If you are doing your job, all your senses are dialed-in each second without exception. You hear or think you see or smell things with your mind as you slip into an imaginative mode. Is it animal or human? Is it the wind or an enemy approaching? A bird swoops down from a nearby tree or flutters about, and your heart cramps tight as if an angina attack is oncoming. The entire team is sound asleep, and you are charged with neither over- nor underreacting. You need to get it right. There is little or no margin of error.

About two hours into my watch, I saw a flicker of light through the jungle web. Well, I thought I saw a light. I also thought my mind might be playing a trick. I kept staring in that direction. I saw it again. Could it be a flashlight? Was that even possible? Would the NVA use a flashlight out in the bush? Not likely, I thought. But we were in their hood, and they probably had no reason to think we were there. I couldn't be too careful. The light started coming closer. Maybe I should wake Sgt. Jacobson. It was the wee hours of the morning. If I were overreacting, he'd be pissed off to a major degree. My heart started to pound. The light was approaching. I grabbed my M79 weapon. *What the fuck is this thing coming at me? Had I waited too long to get help?* It had gotten too close to alert anyone. *We're done; we're done.*

Then the light arrived—a group of fireflies! They flew past me. I let out a long breath while my heart returned to where it anatomically belonged. Those seconds frightened the shit out of me. I knew one thing. I wasn't telling anyone what happened. It would be my secret. If I told anyone, they'd think I was losing it.

* * *

Day two, at 6 a.m., we were back on that same energy-depleting trail. In truth, it was less trail and more a continuous brush battle. The good news was that we hadn't encountered any distractions.

We also knew this path would get us to where we were headed, eventually.

We started up a mountain toward a series of ridges and high terrain. The ground was wet, making the climb plodding and draining. The jungle had become denser and was tearing us up even more. When we weren't getting cut up, we were slipping on mud or climbing over boulders. We rarely took a normal step. Each movement was a struggle. We were moving at a ridiculously slow pace, and it had begun to take a serious toll on us. The sun was beating down, and the humidity was sucking the life out of us. We started to lose patience. Exhaustion had taken over. We had been humping for four hours and had made way less progress than planned.

We stopped. Jacobson, the assistant patrol leader, and I conferred.

Jacobson asked, "What do you guys think? What do you want to do?"

He then said, "Enough of this crap. We need a better way. We'll be worth shit by the time we get to the staging camp."

We knew the choice: battle the elements in a slow grind until we were seriously weakened, but with better safety odds, or find an easier way, preserve some strength, and risk enemy contact and booby traps.

It sounds crazy, but the jungle was often a more formidable opponent than the NVA. The jungle never relented. It couldn't be bowed. It was guaranteed to wear us down. Enemy contact? It might happen or it might not. It was a gamble, and there was always the element of luck.

No question, our physical condition had become a risk factor. For the first time during my tour, my patrol team was in a severely weakened state after less than two days. I cursed the military brass who put us in this position. They couldn't have selected a worse way to get us to the destination. What were they thinking? Were they even?

We could try to stretch the patrol a day or two, but that almost surely meant running out of food and water. And while the pressure to complete the patrol in the designated five days wasn't a direct order, it was as close to an order as there was, a firm unalterable expectation.

We decided to make it easier on ourselves, to rebuild our strength and speed things up, at least for the balance of the day. We would take an easier trail and roll the dice on risk. By best estimates, an easier trail would get us close enough to hunker down near the staging camp for the night so we could execute the prisoner snatch plan the next morning.

We kept the decision to ourselves. We all agreed that nothing would be gained by bringing HQ into the loop. They either wouldn't care, or they'd complicate things. Too many cooks in the kitchen. We were departing from the rules of the road and banking on some luck.

The known risks became evident soon enough. The new trail featured abundant evidence of a population in the general vicinity. The dirt was packed; the leaves and branches were crushed, and every now and then, we came upon footprints. We were moving fast but were increasingly vulnerable each step of the way.

My system of senses for impending danger became heightened the more we advanced. Each smell, sound, and sight magnified. Each step and breath I took focused on the frightening reality that the enemy, with one thing in mind, our destruction, could pop up at anytime and anywhere. I fixated on knowing that life or death could turn on split-second reactions.

I became more conscious of the M79 grenade launcher I was carrying. The M79 had become my weapon of choice on patrols. I had lost faith in the M16, the standard Marine issue. It tended to jam, a tendency that almost got me killed once on a patrol. I had resolved to never again take the M16 with me. The M79, on the other hand, was dependable. Fired typically from the shoulder, it was a single-shot weapon designed to fire grenades full of metal fragments like BBs or a big shotgun shell, also known as a "flew shit" round. It also could fire smoke grenades.

Still, four hours into the day, nothing noteworthy had occurred. Despite the edginess I felt, despite the tension of each moment, it had been business as usual.

Then, without warning or anything happening, I got uneasy. I felt a queasiness in my throat. I darted my eyes everywhere they could reach, looking for something out there. I saw nothing. I heard nothing. I smelled nothing.

I looked down to see fresh boot prints. How recent I wasn't sure. I didn't think we were close to a camp. I slowed to a virtual tippy-toe pace as I came to a bend in the trail beyond which I couldn't see or hear. As I rounded the bend, I looked up, and lo and behold, thirty to forty meters away, in the middle of the trail, stood an NVA soldier looking straight at me. We had made point-to-point contact.

The moment of split-second stillness between us was riveting, emblazoned in my mind. I can still see his belt buckle, uniform, boots, and what he looked like. I also took quick note of his AK-47, which was up. Neither of us had advantage. We both surprised each other. We both were on level ground. Neither had the sun glaring in the eyes. For once, the jungle was neutral. It was a cowboy-like, high-noon moment.

Our eyes locked. Even though his AK-47 was up, I got off my M79 first and hit him. As he stumbled, he got off a volley of rounds with his automatic weapon, the released metal shards zipping above and beside me. Then he hit the ground. I couldn't tell if he was dead.

The exchange broke all hell loose, and in an instant, we were in the shit. We had crossed paths with an NVA patrol team, the size of which was unclear, but likely substantially larger than ours.

Several rounds whistled past me again. I should have been plastered with bullets. Too many rounds missed me to make sense. Did the NVA shoot that poorly? Had divine intervention paid me a timely visit?

Another NVA soldier appeared in my vision, shooting at me with his AK-47. He, too, was all over the place with his aim, again poor accuracy. Or had I become invisible?

The rest of my team arrived and began to set up a perimeter and opened fire. The firefight had started, and it got crazy fast. We hit them hard, trying to create the impression we had more depth than we did.

We needed to buy time. We had to get out of there. We were not equipped for what was unfolding. Once the perimeter got established, it fell to me to create a diversionary situation to allow us to di di mau and get to safer ground. As the firefight ensued, I backed up a few feet to a vantage point. I grabbed a white phosphorus grenade from my bandoleer, what we called a Wilson Pickett or Willy Pete, and loaded it into the M79.

The Willy Pete was a tactical grenade with immediate impact of about ten seconds, sometimes longer. The white phosphorous burnt the skin until the surrounding oxygen feeding the affected areas could be snuffed out. It also blurred vision through the dense, white smoke.

I knelt, put the M79 up along my knee, aimed up and away, and fired the Willy Pete in an arc beyond the perimeter. I watched the grenade make its way to where the enemy had hunkered down. In seconds, the screaming and yelling began from the burn impact, and the smoke created a visibility wall allowing us to haul ass.

We had an aborted operation. Our mission was now survival. While it seemed like a lifetime, within a minute of contact, we had begun running. We moved with a crazed urgency.

I couldn't see but knew our radiomen were all over it getting word to HQ about our predicament, where we were, and that we needed help pronto. My focus shifted to getting the hell out of there, like everyone else. We needed high ground or some safe place, if it existed.

As I took off, I saw another NVA emerge amid the smoke, pointing his AK-47 in my direction. I wasn't invisible after all. I had no time to reload the M79, so I grabbed my .45 pistol and shot at him as I ran. I don't know if I hit him. He missed me.

The smokescreen gave us valuable time. The NVA couldn't know how large a unit they faced. They likely would call for reinforcements, giving us a little more time.

We couldn't run uphill. That would have made us easy to catch. We each instinctively ran downhill, into the ravine—to where, we had no clue.

While running, I continued to fire my .45 while looking over my shoulder, like a cowboy galloping on a horse fleeing an attack on an open, dry prairie, except the conditions were not quite the same. As I fired, with sight on the enemy, I stumbled and tripped. I turned on the ground and fired. I hit an oncoming enemy right in the face, peeling part of it off him, and down he went. I kept running, not dwelling.

I saw my guys at certain times through the trees and bush. At least I thought they were my guys. They were more shadow than person. Whoever they were, they were hauling like me. We were separated and in flight with the enemy in hot pursuit. It was full panic mode, as we were literally running for our lives. All the training didn't mean much. We had to do what we could to survive, which meant running, running fast and running hard, through the triple-canopy, vine-infested, mud-slicked jungle.

People were bouncing off trees, slipping and falling and getting up to run again, deeper and deeper into the ravine. The enemy at once seemed behind, next to, and ahead of us. Both sides had become entangled. It was bedlam. Each at risk of hitting its own. We were scrambling and they were chasing.

The jungle darkness and its difficult terrain made it nearly impossible to get a bead on anyone with any safe degree of identity. Heads bopped ten feet away. But to whom they belonged was not so easy to know. Was it a gray hat (and thus the NVA)? Or was it a green recon boonie hat and one of ours? I didn't always know who was in my line of fire. Sometimes I held fire. Other times, if it looked gray, I'd fire at the shadow and run, not knowing what came of the shot. Fire and keep running. I kept hearing pings here and there, not knowing the source, and not caring. A round is a round, no matter who lets it fly.

I didn't have time to freak out. All I could think of was moving.

I had every confidence our radiomen were doing everything imaginable to find help, but they were doing it on the run, not knowing where we were headed, struggling to be precise with coordinates, while fearing for their lives. I was desperately trying to keep an eye on them because, of all the options, and they were precious few, staying close to the radiomen gave me the best chance of survival. Where were they? I couldn't hear them. I couldn't see them. I had to find them as I ran. They were our sole lifeline.

It had become each man for himself. We had scattered as a team, each running with urgency to a place called nowhere, in and out of trees, over rocks, through bushes, down the muddy slopes, hoping against hope we didn't run flat into a tree, get felled, and become easy pickings. My eyes continued to scan terrain to make sure I didn't fall or run into the shadows of others doing the same thing, both enemy and fellow patrol members.

I have this memory of a banyan tree with gargantuan roots that almost grabbed my feet and tossed me down. Somehow, I dodged its tentacles.

There was no front, back, or in-between.

The jungle had long since humbled me. Now it was destroying me.

I had competed in major races as a runner. I had survived Marine Corps Boot Camp. I had received gut-wrenching recon training. I had been in-country several months battling the jungle and cheating death. I thought I was indestructible and perhaps a little lucky. But none of it prepared me for this situation, running for my life amid the worst the jungle had to inflict. No dress rehearsal could prepare us for what we faced.

Tumbling through the sharp-edged brush, I could hear the tearing of my jungle fatigues and feel the slashing of my skin and blood running down my arm.

In the madness, I realized that collectively we had at most enough ammo for several minutes of engaged exchanges and that, at some point, if we could somehow reassemble, one final stand left in us. Otherwise, the enemy would pick us off one at a time. We couldn't run indefinitely.

The ravine kept descending with seemingly no end in sight. The terrain was steep and powerful. It was as if the heart of the jungle had a magnetic force pulling us deeper into its vortex— and toward our final fate.

I struggled to keep my eyes on other members of the patrol. Shots continued to ring out. Had the radiomen made contact? Was help on the way? Was I going to die soon? Should I stop and confront the enemy and die an honorable death? If not, would I die while running away, taking a round in the back of the head or through the heart?

I started to think: How much time did I have left to live? How did I want to die?

The slope was narrowing. It seemed I was headed to the bottom of the ravine and who knows what. The narrower it got, the more eagerly my eyes scanned for team members. I could hear shuffling in the bushes. The shooting behind me had stopped.

And then, I saw Marines, one at time, each moving toward the same point. The canyon had funneled us back together. Miracle of miracles. Everyone was alive. Everyone had made it to the same spot through an insane dash for survival.

My exhilaration at seeing everyone, however, wore off quickly, giving way to the scary feeling that this would indeed be our last stand. Everything stopped for me. I froze for a second. I saw the future. *We're gonna die.*

Yes, we would fight and die as a unit. The jungle had delivered us to our joint burial ground. The jungle did have some empathy. It did show us some consideration.

You fought and patrolled together. You will now die together.

A huge welcoming bomb crater came into sight, like an oasis springing from the desert floor. Embedded between us and the crater, however, lay a huge mud-filled rice patty. The only way to safety, temporary and fragile as it might be, was to trudge through the deep mud, as high as our knees, dragging leg after leg, the mud yanking on our boots, moving in excruciating short intervals, frightened the entire time, wondering how much time we could remain in the open before getting picked off. In those vital seconds, dodging a bullet was not an option. If the NVA opened fire while we were stuck in the mud, each of us would be target practice, praying the enemy had poor marksmanship.

We got there. The crater measured about ten feet in diameter and a few feet deep. It was overgrown, full of stagnant water, and home to various jungle denizens, including leeches. Beyond the patties and the crater, the thick jungle resumed. Locals had carved out this section to grow food. Then U.S. forces bombed the hell out of it, leaving the crater as its signature. It wasn't much, but the crater had become our cathedral sanctuary—at least for the time being.

We built a perimeter with what claymores remained, spreading them equidistant five feet from the edge of the crater. Normally, we'd place them twenty feet out. But we had decent cover where we were, and bringing our sorry asses beyond five feet, up the slope slightly, would expose us more. We didn't want to get too far out there and gift the enemy sight on us. We frankly couldn't afford anyone getting hit before the final battle. We knew we were soon to face grossly disproportionate numbers. We needed to be at full force, such as it was.

The primary radioman—our most powerful weapon at this point—was active, trying to contact someone. I didn't get any comfort from the panic in his face. Sgt. Jacobson and the assistant patrol leader were next to him, riveted on maps, helping with coordinates. We had outrun the enemy, and they had stopped coming at us. I knew—we all knew—they were preparing for a major and final assault. They knew where the slope took us. They knew we were holed up in the crater waiting for them. We were where they wanted us.

One thing we also knew, and they did too: they had to come downhill at us. They would be exposed. It gave us an early advantage.

Still, the NVA were a known quantity in this war. They were fighting for something that burned deep and long in their hearts. This wasn't a boundary war. This was a cultural-political war for all the marbles. It meant they would risk lives to overrun us. They had to be amassing in numbers. They would come at us with everything they could summon.

It was simply a matter of the math. We had maybe five minutes of ammunition left. Five minutes to delay them, slow them down. Five minutes to live once they came down the slope.

The whispers among us dripped with the worst kind of destiny. All hope seemingly had vanished. In the absence of help, we were done. Some started to pray. I kept looking out there, looking for movement. I wasn't going down easily. I wanted my Alamo moment.

We said our goodbyes, some with words, some with eyes.

Someone asked the corpsman how much morphine we had available. The question gave me a shudder. I understood though. I could see electing suicide by overdose rather than succumbing to death at the hands of the enemy or becoming a prisoner of war. It wasn't my way. But I understood how that question could be asked, and I respected it. To his credit, the corpsman shut down the discussion before it began with a "let's wait and see" response.

We were locked and loaded, holding fire, knowing we needed to make every fired round count. We couldn't afford to fire into an area. We didn't have any ammunition to waste and the luxury of time to miss. If we fired, it had to be to hit a specific target. We had to wait until the enemy got exposed. It was our Bunker Hill, Revolutionary War moment: "Don't fire until you see the whites of their eyes." So, we waited, the next minutes passing in silence.

I glanced around. Some had heads down, doubtless praying or pleading with whatever powers they recognized.

I knew what some were still thinking. I knew it because I was thinking it. If we get overrun, do we go down fighting? Is the white flag an option? Do we surrender before getting slaughtered? Or do we end our own lives rather than be killed by the NVA?

The eyes around provided the answer, speaking volumes. We are afraid and we are ready. We aren't succumbing. Bring it on. *We're going down fighting.*

The radiomen were communicating constantly. Finally, they reported that two CH-46s were en route to extract us. Our hearts soared. We got focused on extraction. Our hearts soared higher when we heard the delightful *whup-whup-whup* sound of chopper wings nearing us. We were getting the hell out of there. We'd live another day.

Then the *whup-whup* became fainter, and the first radioman reported that the CH-46s were pulling out, that HQ had ordered them to leave because they were taking too much fire. That, in a nutshell, meant HQ didn't want to risk the helicopter squads and the two machines to save a recon team so deep in the shit that they faced a high probability of death or capture.

Talk about deflating a balloon. We were fucked.

Then a savior appeared. The Purple Foxes, evidently not too far away, decided to ignore the orders. They didn't give a shit. "We're coming in. Get us some cover." A Bronco was dispatched to provide cover, and when they arrived, they tossed a smoke grenade to "pop a smoke" to get vision on us.

The sounds shattered the silence that shrouded us, a constant stream of *rat-tat-tat-tat* that appeared like horizonal raindrops penetrating the jungle, pinging tree bark, leaves, brush, and the moist jungle carpet. I raised my eyes to see the winged, twin-turboprop OV-10 Bronco aircraft, with its light attack weaponry, swooping down toward the rice patties, pelting the jungle with a stream of firepower. The radioman turned to me and said excitedly, "Does he see us? Does the fucker see us?" I didn't know if the pilot had sight of us. But I knew this, help had arrived. I basked in the sweet sounds of the Bronco Gatling gun rounds ripping up the jungle, keeping the enemy at bay, providing us cover, and, best of all, gifting us time to live.

Then more help came. As the Bronco kept pummeling the forest, two Cobra birds arrived and fired two rockets into the congested jungle areas. The explosion of the rockets gave me a full-body rush I'd never felt before. Our artillery had made its presence known in a big way. The Cobras' arrival gave the Bronco the green light to leave. It had done its job and passed the baton to the Cobras. God love them!

For the first time, we knew we had a chance to survive the insanity. Hope had returned. It wasn't over, though. We still had to get extracted, and that depended on the ability of the Purple Foxes and their CH-46s to get there in time and find a place to land.

Less than two minutes later, our ultimate saviors arrived, two from the Purple Fox squadron. One stayed high keeping an eye on things; the other had the more dangerous role of extracting us. Both were firing machine gun rounds into the jungle.

Our next problem was that the CH-46 couldn't land anywhere near us. To retrieve us, the chopper would have to drop a ladder for us to climb up and harness into what we called our Swiss saddle. Once secured on the ladder, we would hang in the sky, exposed the whole way back to base camp.

And so it went. One at a time, we climbed and clamped. The last man was the primary radioman, who was coordinating on the ground with the pilot. All the while, the Purple Fox gunners gave us superb cover spraying the area with their machine guns until we were high enough to be out of danger.

Hanging and Hoping

We were removed from battle. We were spectators, our fate placed squarely in the good hands of the CH-46 crew. We couldn't do any better than that. I cherished each second we were in the sky, holding on tightly, rising higher toward the clouds.

I'll never forget the moment we touched down at Camp Reasoner. I felt reborn. We had beaten back the Grim Reaper of the Vietnam War. Incredibly, other than jungle damage and depletions of our souls, we were unscathed. No one had a single enemy-induced wound.

I don't how many rounds missed me. But it was quite a few. Sgt. Jacobson began to call me "the Ghost." I'll go with that.

We would later learn from the CH-46 crew that the reinforced enemy numbers were in the range of one hundred. We didn't stand a chance.

The reaction at home base was nonchalant. It was along the lines of: "Okay, you guys fucked up. You're lucky to be alive. Get a hot meal and a shower, and we'll talk in a couple of days."

From a military perspective, the mission was a failure. We never reached our destination and never got what we were charged with securing. It's hard to quarrel with that conclusion. But we emerged alive when we seemed as good as dead. That struck me, and still does, as a fair measure of what success means.

The heroics of our comrades manning the Bronco, Cobra, and Purple Fox aircraft can never be overstated. Their timely arrival, bravery, and extraordinary skill gave us our lives back.

I have heard stories of people literally coming back from the dead, where their hearts stopped, yet miraculously made their way back. I don't know what that feels like, but I will say this. As I hung in the sky in my Swiss saddle, with the jungle growing more distant, I had a sense of what it might be like to return from death. The farther we got from that bomb crater, the more exhilarated I felt. I was going to live another day.

THE ORPHANAGE

Kindness is giving hope to those who
think they are all alone in this world.
— Lewis Brownlee

O f all the things I'd seen and endured in Vietnam, the good,
the bad, and the horrific, one experience found a warm and
lasting place in my heart. A village near Camp Reasoner
had an orphanage for Vietnamese children, and as the ravaging
war continued, its numbers multiplied day by day, creating a col-
lateral consequence of profound sadness. To make things worse,
the orphanage suffered from a devastating lack of resources. They
had virtually nothing, and the adults who cared for the children
often resorted to begging or stealing food. Only the hardest of
hearts wouldn't be moved by the situation.

We developed a grand plan to raise funds and obtain dona-
tions of clothing and food to lend a hand. Astonishingly, the military chaplain turned down our efforts to help, with the excuse
that as a "Christian," he couldn't see his way to help "Buddhists."
As I said, the hardest of hearts. I tried again, this time seeking
the assistance of my church at home in Novato, California, only
again to be turned away because the children and their adult care-
takers were Buddhists. I sought the advice of my mother, and

she encouraged me to write to people I knew at home, whether they supported the war or not. She felt that political views notwithstanding, people at home would instinctively open their hearts—and their wallets—to help those poor (and innocent) kids. I did what I could and waited with fingers crossed.

After I returned, depleted physically and emotionally, from a several-day mission in the jungle, I learned that a truckload of food and clothing had arrived from California for the orphanage. My most fervent wish had been filled. I was overwhelmed and shed tears of joy. The people succeeded where the government had failed and abandoned them. We had made a difference, perhaps a tiny one, but a positive impact on the lives of children who were a distinct class of unspoken victims of the war in Vietnam.

Some of the children we tried to help

— 18 —

P.S.

> Without memory, there is no healing.
> Without forgiveness, there is no future.
> — Desmond Tutu

The following are excerpts plucked out of sequence from letters I wrote home from Vietnam. They represent what life was like for me as a combat Marine.

* * *

"Haven't seen the sun or the stars these couple of weeks. It just keeps raining. At least it isn't cold. But I'd welcome seeing some stars or even the moon once in a while."

* * *

"Last week we killed some weird snake. It was at least 12 feet long and was 4 inches or more around. It was huge. I was one of the guys that helped kill it. It took four of us to carry it. I was ashamed we killed it. The snake was just lying on the side of the trail, under a fallen tree, not bothering anyone."

* * *

"When we go out into the field, we wear our jungle outfit + camouflage on our faces. I look like a walking tree, maybe you'd like
me in your garden."

* * *

"One has to be involved with [the war] to understand what it is
all about."

* * *

"There is something you can send in your next package, if you
will. 3 lg cans of Rock Ape food, we're getting low. Some cat food
for the tigers, peanuts for the elephants, and some blood for the
leeches, I'm running out. And maybe a stick of salami for the kid."

* * *

"It's not just jungle like, it is the real true for real jungle, with all
kinds of weird noises and sounds."

* * *

I tell ya these [VC] guys are real lousy shooters. They put their
rifles on automatic; start shooting, they're so small that the rifle takes them all over. It looks like they're doing some kind of
dance, with the rifle climbing up over their head and rounds racing to the moon, not coming near us. Thank-God no one taught
them how to shoot. That day we got 7 confirmed KIAs and 12
possible."

* * *

"Three seasons: 1. Monsoon season, 2. The rainy season. 3. The
wet season. Would you believe I [am] starting to resemble a
duck?"

*   *   *

"I sometimes wonder when Tarzan is going to be coming flying out of the trees with a banana hanging out of his mouth + pounding his chest, asking us 'Where's Jane?'"

*   *   *

"Many things about the war I'm against."

*   *   *

"Never boring."

*   *   *

"On our last patrol, it was supposed to be a 7-day humper. We got pulled out by ladder on our 4th day. We found all kinds of groovy things, like caves, punji stick factory, base camp, and finally we got a prisoner."

*   *   *

"The Rock Apes give us more trouble than the enemy does."

*   *   *

Chased for 6 hours through the jungle, our point man broke his leg jumping boulders. And since we were behind a big mountain range, we lost communication. So we carried our point to high ground to get communication, just to get ourselves surrounded."

*   *   *

"We've been going out and doing our job (getting enemy information). Our team brought back a prisoner."

* * *

"Well the Rock Apes are really something else. It seems we're fight[ing] Rock Apes more than the enemy."

* * *

"It was so wet out there. I was on my rear end more than my feet, flying or should I say sliding down hills and riverbeds. So they decided to walk trails. I almost shit my pants. I found 2 punji pits, after that patrol I was a nervous wreck, but now I'm A.P.O (assistant patrol leader), so I don't have to walk point anymore. Someone up there loves me."

* * *

"We had a few men wounded and only 2 men got killed this month."

* * *

"The prisoner [we captured today] said the reason that Da Nang wasn't hit hard in the Tet Offensive was cause 'Recon would find our position, call in air support or artillery and blow us up or find our supply lines and blow them up.'"

* * *

"Sure didn't want to worry anyone back home, but I must admit it feels good to know that somebody worries about me."

* * *

"At times [the NVA] were closer than 50 meters from us firing to see if we'd shoot back, that way they could locate us easier. So we just tossed grenades at them, that way they can't tell where we're at."

* * *

"The other night we harbored up on top of Lil Hill, set in for the night. Finally, when it got dark we realized we set in on top of a giant ant hill. That night we got overrun by ants. Them Lil creepy crawlers were everywhere. The problem was, once it gets dark, at night, no way can ya move at night, the danger is far too great, so we let them ants play with us all night. I can finally say that I had ants up my pants."

* * *

"When in the bush, we eat one meal a day, so we kind of enjoy it no matter if its good or not."

* * *

"We have had a couple of casualties, not from Rock Apes or the enemy, but from tigers, one guy became cat food, don't really understand. Tigers don't really like human meat, unless they're real old and can't catch their chow."

* * *

"All we do when we're back into the area is drink beer, we have beer for breakfast, lunch, dinner, and for a bedtime snack."

* * *

"The Rock Apes have something going for them. When they get mad + have a dispute, they throw rocks. I think I'd rather be overseas throwing rocks at each other than shooting bullets."

* * *

"Over here it rains one day then the next it's 90°."

* * *

"The terrain is wet and muddy. The Rock Apes like it wet and muddy. At times I wish I were a Rock Ape."

* * *

"There are times you'd wish Vietnam wasn't here on this earth."

* * *

"Not sure where I'm headed, but I'm leaving, that's all I really care about."

* * *

The following are excerpts from the final letter I sent home, addressed to "Civilians, Friends, Draft Dodgers, etc." It was in the spirit of an instructional guide for everyone who might have the misfortune of dealing with me as I transitioned to civilian life. I urged everyone to make "certain allowances for the crude environment, which has been [my] miserable lot for the past twelve months."

* * *

"Show no alarm if [I insist] on carrying a weapon to the dinner table, look around for [my] steel pot when offered a chair, or wake you up in the middle of the night for guard duty."

"Pretend not to notice when [I eat] with [my] fingers instead of silverware and prefer C-rations to steak."

"Take it with a smile when [I insist] on digging up the garden to fill sandbags for the bunker [I'm] building."

"Be tolerant when [I take] the blanket and sheets off [my] bed and put them on the floor to sleep."

"Abstain from saying anything about powdered eggs, dehydrated potatoes, fried rice, fresh milk, or ice cream."

"Do not be alarmed if [I] jump up from the dinner table and rush to the garbage can to wash [my] dish with a toilet brush."

"If it should start raining, pay no attention to [me] if [I pull] off [my] clothes, grab a bar of soap and a towel, and run outdoors for a shower."

"Pretend not to notice if at a restaurant [I call] waitresses 'numbah one Girls' and [use my] hat as an ashtray."

"Simply leave quickly and calmly if by some chance [I] utter 'didi' with an irritated look on [my] face, because it means no less 'than get the hell out of here.'"

"Above all, keep in mind that beneath that tanned and rugged exterior there is a heart of gold (the only thing of value [I have] left). Treat with kindness, tolerance, and an occasional 5th of good liquor, and you will be able to rehabilitate that which was once (and is now the hollow shell of) the happy-go-lucky guy you once knew and loved."

"The KID is coming home! ! ! !"

BY THE NUMBERS

> The first bomb, the first explosion, burst in our hearts.
> —Erich Maria Remarque, *All Quiet on the Western Front*

I saw their faces
Our eyes locked together
Their uniform pockets
Had
Letters and Photos
Family and Friends
Same as mine
Close to our hearts
IDs too
They were19
So was I
We were the same
I saw the guys I killed
I had killed me

— Darren Walton

Below are some statistics. Buried inside them lie countless untold stories, many unknowable and many most of us might not want to know. I hope they get told somehow, somewhere, in some fashion, and I hope those affected find a way out of their personal tragedies or still can, as I continue to try to do.

The numbers below, by themselves, tell their own story. They tell of pervasive and wanton destruction, profound human pain, and emotional isolation. They represent a repulsive legacy that will indelibly darken humanity. They need no embellishment to still the heart and shock the conscience.

- **2.7 million** Americans served in uniform in Vietnam.
- **58,148** Americans were killed in action (KIA) in Vietnam (including medic Thomas P. Coffino, the brother of the co-author of this book).
- Of those Americans KIA, the average age was **twenty-three**; more than **60 percent** were **twenty or younger**; five were **sixteen**; the oldest was **sixty-two**; and more than **17,000** were married.
- It is estimated that almost **300,000** Vietnam veterans eventually **died** from Agent Orange exposure during the war.
- **2,338** Americans were missing in action; more than **1,600** are unaccounted for today.
- **766** Americans became prisoners of war (POW) and of them, **114** died in captivity.
- More than **303,000** Americans were wounded.
- More than **75,000** American soldiers were severely disabled as a result of the war. More than **5,200** lost limbs, and more than **1,000** suffered multiple amputations.
- Countless Vietnam veterans have committed suicide.
- One study shows that almost **20 percent** of Vietnam veterans returned with post-traumatic stress disorder (PTSD).
- Between **200,000 and 250,000** South Vietnamese soldiers died in the war.

- Approximately **4.8 million** Vietnamese were exposed to Agent Orange contamination during the war, of whom **400,000** have died from the exposure.
- More than **300,000** Vietnamese "boat people" trying to flee Vietnam either died or were killed by pirates.
- As many as **2,000,000** Vietnamese civilians (North and South) and about **1,100,000** North Vietnamese and Viet Cong soldiers died during the war.
- South Korea suffered more than **4,000** dead, Thailand about **350**, Australia more than **500**, and New Zealand some **three dozen.**
- The number of families from all affected countries that were devastated is **countless.**

EPILOGUE

> Keep your face to the sunshine and
> you cannot see a shadow.
> — Helen Keller

I didn't know what to expect, transitioning from war to life at home. I certainly didn't anticipate that the bridge forward would be as bumpy as it was, and for sure I didn't have an inkling that the climb out of madness would never quite end. The reality became clear: once war gets ahold of you, it tends not to let go.

I returned to what I had hoped would be a routine life in Marin County, California, where I was raised. Before too long, while attending the College of Marin (COM), courtesy of the G.I. Bill), I shared a house in San Rafael with two high school running buddies, Bob Bunnell and Dave Stancliffe. Bob and I were members of the COM cross-country team, along with the late and irrepressible Robin Williams, who often hung out with us. We maintained a relaxed and fun atmosphere, which meant beer, pot, and trips to San Francisco for rock concerts. It was 1972, and, on the surface, all was good.

As stated in the preface, I tried to hide my combat duty experience. I didn't want people to know I was a Marine who fought in

Vietnam. I didn't want to deal with how they might react when they discovered I served in combat in the controversial war. Being a Vietnam War veteran at the time was, to put it mildly, unpopular, and in many social circles demoted you to persona non grata, especially in the politically progressive Marin County culture. I wanted people to deal with me based on who I knew I was, not through an unforgiving lens that abhorred the military. I respected the anti-war point of view. I just didn't want people to flog me with it. And so, wherever I gathered socially, I repressed my military background, my version of don't ask, don't tell.

But keeping others in the dark about my background didn't mean I could escape myself. That much I learned the hard way—with nightmares.

Each time a nightmare descended, I found myself alone in the sweltering triple-canopy jungle. Each time it was daytime and dark, and I was running full throttle through the bush, fleeing some unknown and invisible force. In every nightmare, I ran in fear and was consumed with panic, desperately trying to survive and live another day. I never stopped running as I navigated the jungle labyrinth, not daring to look over my shoulder to get a glimpse of what was behind me and whether it was gaining ground. I ran without destination, other than away from whatever it was I was running from. The entire time my heart beat heavily, and my body oozed sweat. I never got caught or overrun. I ran and ran and ran until I awoke, sweating, breathing heavily, gasping for air, and praying I was now safe.

The nightmares didn't have a predictable timetable. They'd happen every now and then. And while they might abate for a time, they'd always return. They didn't let me be alone for too long. I don't worry about them anymore. They are part of my life, my psyche, who I am.

While the nightmares came and went, another reminder of ghosts past took an even firmer hold on me, as it related to daily life.

I returned from Vietnam with a duffle bag full of what most people would consider memorabilia. I stored the bag in my bedroom closet, and because it had a sliding glass door, the duffle bag was continuously visible in the room, certainly to me.

Looking back, I am not sure why I kept the damn thing. But I did, and it served as a constant reminder of where I'd been for two long years. Worse, my eyes habitually fixated on the bag, especially when I'd step into the closet for something, triggering a constellation of memories of thirteen life-threatening months in the southeast Asian jungle. Sometimes the exhumed memories would stay with me the balance of the day, like a haunting shadow.

The duffle bag came to symbolize my time as a combat Marine, a reminder of a part of my life I wanted to forget.

After a year of self-induced torture, I decided I'd had enough.

I didn't want to dump the bag and its contents into the garbage, although I confess that option crossed my mind. I had enough residual respect for military service not to travel down that road. But I had to rid my life of that bag and in a way that eliminated or greatly reduced the gnawing effect of jungle war experiences.

One fall afternoon, instinctively, and admittedly with rising anger, I liberated the duffle bag from the closet, tossed it into the back of my car, and, after grabbing a Ka-Bar and an entrenching tool, made my way to the beach. En route I stopped at a deli and picked up a sandwich, lighter fluid, matches, and a bottle of Jack Daniels. All set.

About thirty minutes later, I arrived at my destination, Limantour Beach, a part of Point Reyes National Seashore, with a stretch of four miles of beach and low sand dunes. Limantour is beautiful and, not surprisingly, quite popular among locals, especially families. Because of the time of year and day, however, I assumed the beach would be deserted, and it was.

The plan was to burn the duffle bag contents ceremoniously so I could get on with my life.

After parking the car, I retrieved a blanket, the duffle bag, and my deli acquisitions and walked north on the beach to find an isolated spot near the dunes. By the time I found a suitable location, it was nearing 5 p.m. The sky was clear, the sun edging toward the horizon. The ocean breezes had picked up, and a fog bank crept along the ocean's edge. Gorgeous.

I took a seat mid-beach in the sand, not too far from the tideline, and stared straight ahead. I often sat on Northern California beaches. It was a familiar space for me. I felt at home.

I collected some firewood from the dunes and started a fire. When the fire took hold, I began eating the sandwich and taking long pulls from the bottle of Jack Daniels. I warmed up quickly.

Not too long after getting comfortable, I began to remove articles from the bag, including dress greens and utilities, and started cutting them into pieces with the Ka-Bar. As I shredded the clothes, I tossed items one at a time into the fire. Watching them get consumed with flames put me in a trance, and I continued the ceremony methodically, cutting and tossing, cutting and tossing. Sparks rose, which speckled the curtain backdrop of the sky beautifully as light gave way to darkness.

I enjoyed watching the fire consume my uniforms. I tracked sparks as they rose and dissolved in the sky, each time feeling a rush of satisfaction. Was I being purged incrementally of stains on my soul? Hard to say. But I felt good, mindful that I was steadily imbibing whiskey as well. But the more sparks and ash integrated into the horizon against the backdrop of the pounding surf, the more enthralled I became. It was hypnotic.

I burned everything I had, including T-shirts, dress uniforms, utilities, collared shirts, and camouflage pants. The exception was my bush hat and boots. I didn't want to burn those. Was it nostalgia? Pride? A connection I didn't want to sever? I don't know. I still have them. Both bear the same reminders as the duffle bag. But they are different from the other items. I wore both virtually each day in the jungle. They were symbols of survival. They became part of my identity. I can't give them up.

As the last items burned, the sun set, and night was upon me. I returned the bush hat and my boots to the duffle bag. I leaned back and closed my eyes. I felt sated.

The next thing I remember is waking up on the cusp of the dunes as the sun was rising the next morning. I had slept the entire night on the beach! I was wearing a jacket and wrapped in a blanket. The fire pit was gone. The tide had taken all traces of what I had done—and part of my past—out to sea.

After the ceremony at Limantour, I went on with my life. I never told anybody about what happened that night at the beach until recently, decades later, when I told my wife Gina as we discussed the idea of writing this book. I worried people would think that cutting and burning a military uniform was akin to burning the flag, which would put me in a select group whose membership I didn't want. When I told Gina, she urged me to include the Limantour ceremony in this book. She reasoned that the beach episode was a key part of my story and who I am. She had a point. I'm not saying it was right, wrong, good, or bad, only that it was something I felt compelled to do almost fifty years ago to help cleanse my soul. How effective was the cleansing? Hard to say. But I survived to talk about it, and that counts for something.

I still visit Limantour, but in truth, I've never returned to the spot of the fire. I felt that what I did back then was important for me to do, but once done, I wanted to move on. It was designed to help me forget, put things out of my life, and to some extent, it worked. It purged some of the darkness that the Vietnam War had stamped on my soul, and for that I am grateful.

The cleansing by fire wasn't a cure, of course. I sensed that then and know that now. The transition continues, one painful step at a time. The war experience is perpetual. I get that. The nightmares have not gone away, although, thankfully, they are less frequent, less unsettling. We Vietnam veterans are locked in spirit and pain for all time. I can live with that.

Boots and Bush Hat: Vestiges of the Past Still with Me

ACKNOWLEDGMENTS

> When eating fruit, remember who planted the tree.
> — Vietnamese proverb

As I gaze down the long tunnel of my past and ponder the ramp up to this book, it is hard to know where to begin to thank the many people who kept me alive and helped pave the way for this project to launch and finish. Countless people whose names I've long forgotten deserve recognition. I only wish I could identify them and express my gratitude publicly.

It's easy to forget soldiers fighting in wars far, far away from home. Citizens removed from the fray of battle have lives to lead, differing interests, and responsibilities. During wartime, we veterans often are out of sight, out of mind. I understand.

But the truth is, when I served my thirteen-month tour in Vietnam, I knew that many people cared. They sent word in letters and love in packages and emoted good karmic energy from their hearts, giving us hope, making us feel cherished and, most of all, not forgotten.

I owe them.

So many nurses, for example, toiled under deplorable conditions, fighting the odds each day to mend us and save our lives, not to mention how much they listened to our rants, ramblings, and crying bouts and comforted us with heartfelt kindness. They asked for nothing in return. They were saints, and while their names may be long forgotten, they each occupy a permanent and appreciative place in my heart. Thank you all.

There were, of course, the corpsmen, our personal doctors in residence, whose singular mandate was unshakeable: to save our lives and keep us as patched together as humanely possible in those godforsaken jungle conditions. It wasn't always possible. Their role as savior at times succumbed to horrific conditions, beyond their capacity to fill. But their devotion to their mission never wavered, not for a second, no matter how hairy it got, no matter how much circumstances imperiled their own lives. Thank you, fellow Marines.

The same was true for the chopper pilots and their crews, whose courage in my lifetime remains unmatched. How amazing to have these strangers standing by to extract us from danger. No matter that they, too, could die in their efforts, they always had our backs. A deep bow to all of them.

I have to thank my mother, who is still kicking, and I mean kicking, and my late father, for the many sacrifices they both made for my brother and me to enjoy a comfortable and inspired childhood. My father, I want to note, fought in WWII in the Battle of Okinawa. He got wounded and received the Purple Heart and returned home to tell us about it. His brother, my Uncle LaMoyne, was not so fortunate. A member of the vaunted Carlson Raiders, the predecessors of Marine recon, he succumbed in the Battle of Tarawa, considered one of the bloodiest and costliest battles in WWII, killing about a thousand Marines and Navy sailors, with more than two thousand wounded. Semper fi, Uncle LaMoyne.

A big shout out to Jerry Weinhold, with whom I shared many a warm moment in Camp Reasoner after recon missions when life seemed possible. Jerry was a radioman extraordinaire and gave my coauthor and me keen insight into how he saw that role as part of Marine reconnaissance. Thank you, Jerry, for your friendship—and your exemplary service.

Along with Jerry Weinhold, Greg Kenyon and J. L. Wiley (to whom this book is dedicated) were my true war buddies and best friends during my tour. They accepted me unconditionally into their inner circle, even after they learned I hailed from the off-center state of California and even worse from San Francisco. Marines, at least the ones I knew, looked askance at those of us from the world of the flower child. But not Greg and J. L. They embraced me as a brother and made me feel welcome.

Bob Bunnell, Ron Elijah, and Don Makela, with whom I grew up and who were my running buddies, deserve mention as the few who were willing to listen to my Vietnam stories after I came home when no one else would. They, unlike many others, gave me the time of day. Thanks, gentlemen.

Thank you, Jane Fairweather Williams and Derry Elijah Bunnell, two fellow Marin County denizens who never forgot me, regularly sending letters and packages not only to me but also to my fellow recon Marines who did not enjoy the same degree of remembrance and attention from family and friends back home. Both of you infused a sense of home and warmth into our often-dreary jungle lives. I cannot tell you how uplifting it was to get something from home. It made me feel prized and allowed me to forget, if but for a limited time, where I was and what I faced.

Thank you also to Bill Rule and his mother, Dolly, who also sent packages and became custodian of the many letters I wrote from Vietnam and used for this book.

Dennis Welch is a high school buddy and decorated Marine chopper gunner who flew with the Purple Foxes at the same time they were saving my sorry ass. I did not learn until I got home that Dennis served at the same time and that, most likely, he had extracted my unit more than once from the jungle after a recon mission. Dennis is an American hero. He also kindly contributed to this book by sitting for a couple of interviews. Thanks, brother.

Thank you, Gordy Evans, an OV10 Bronco pilot, and his talented aerial observer Michael Cerre, for sitting for an interview for this book and, more so, for finding and saving the lives of recon teams.

Thank you, Frank Archibald, a.k.a. "Archie," a fellow Marine grunt who many times put his life on the line to help save the rest of us. Archie also graciously sat for an interview for this book. Many thanks as well for your time, wisdom, and insight.

John Sammons, my Marin County neighbor who, it turned out, was a Navy intelligence officer serving in Vietnam and who might have been responsible for crafting some of our recon missions, deserves thanks. John not only sat with my coauthor and me for interviews, but he helped decipher the mysteries of the recon missions and got me to understand the complexity and thoughtfulness behind them, disarming me from the deep resentment I had about those responsible for shaping our military excursions. John provided invaluable support for the book, not the least of which is the stunning photo of the Rock Ape.

I bow to the unmatched Sgt. Michael Larkins, a real badass Marine, who was my patrol leader and who made decisions that no man should ever have to make in a lifetime. Like others I've mentioned, he saved my life and those of many others by virtue of his leadership and fortitude. Sarge, I will never forget you. Thanks for your bravery. Sgt. Larkins also sat for an interview for the book, helping to shape that incredible chapter on the tiger in the wild.

Sean Stevens, counselor at the Marin County Veterans Service Office, himself a combat soldier, helped many of us find our way forward from the darkness in our souls and the cracks in our sanity. Thank you, Sean, for your kindness and support. Another hero in my eyes.

To Courtney Valdez, another veteran counselor, thank you as well for the many hours of hard work you devoted to helping us weary and troubled veterans. I know it wasn't easy dealing with us. It had to be an enormous challenge at times, but you never stopped caring for us. You never stopped trying to make us better. I am forever grateful to you. You, too, are a hero.

Thank you, Anna Leaf, a Navy nurse during the Vietnam War, who saved the lives of many Marines returning home. As the book recounts, I first met her husband, Dennis Leaf, a Marine officer, as part of the amazing race in Vietnam. My coauthor found Anna after a long search, and we hoped to interview Dennis for the book, only to learn that he had died of lung cancer a few years earlier. Anna gave us her time and many photos, as well as put us in touch with several of Dennis's friends and fellow runners. Anna is also a hero.

Thank you, Colonel Mike Fallon, my commanding officer while in 1st Recon, for all the information and time and sage editing suggestions you gave us from that encyclopedic mind of yours. Col. Fallon personifies Marine.

Thank you to brothers Paul and Kenn Costanzo for the beautiful work you did helping with the book cover. Paul handled the original calligraphy, and Kenn, through KZO Productions.com, handled the cover art and design.

Thank you, friends of Dennis Leaf and fellow long-distance runners Alan Steifel, R. C. Miller (also a Marine officer who ran against me in the Vietnam Olympics), Tim Yanacheck, and Walter Wilowatyj for allowing us to plumb your backgrounds and experiences with Dennis. Much appreciated.

Thank you, Dave McSorley (Marine chopper pilot), Larry Snee (Marine recon point man), and Doc Thurman (Marine corpsman) for graciously giving us your time and sharing your war experiences to help with this book.

I owe a deep measure of thanks to my coauthor Michael J. Coffino, now a true buddy, without whom this book would not have happened. I needed his writing skills and constant sage advice. Hey, Michael, thanks for believing in me and making this happen.

And last but most certainly not least, I want to express my love and gratitude to my wife, Gina, as tough and sharp as any Marine, who stood by me during the many years that I suffered from PTSD and who tolerated the rollercoaster ride I took in writing this book. Thank you, Gina, also for the support you gave me day in and day out, in the form of input, ideas, disagreements, a good pair of ears and, sometimes, tough love. You are extraordinary.

Semper fi.

ABOUT THE AUTHORS

DARREN WALTON

Darren was born and raised and still lives in Marin County, California, which he cherishes for its extraordinary coastline, sprawling open spaces, diverse terrains, and sheer beauty. He has been a long-distance runner since high school and continues to run the hills and mountains of California on a regular basis. Recently, he organized and led the first group of over-seventy runners to compete in the grueling Hood to Coast long-distance running in Oregon, which stunned the assembled runners and public with their impressive performance.

After his stint in the Marines, Darren pursued a variety of endeavors and ran multiple businesses, including as a commercial diver, locomotive engineer, and personal gym trainer. He currently owns and operates a machine shop in San Rafael, California, called Walton's Saw Works, which was founded in 1956 and specializes in sales and services of router bits, saw blades, and printer's knives, among other items.

Darren lives with his wife, Gina, in Marin County, California, and has a son, Andy.

MICHAEL J. COFFINO

Before becoming a full-time author, ghostwriter, and freelance editor, Michael had two parallel careers: one in the courtroom and the other in the gymnasium. He was a business litigation and trial attorney and legal writing instructor for more than four decades and concurrently devoted twenty-five years as a basketball coach, primarily at the high school level.

He has written or coauthored eight published books, including *Truth Is in the House*, his debut novel.

Michael grew up in the South Bronx. He served in the U.S. Army 1968–1970 and later earned a BS in Education from the City University of New York and a JD from the University of California, Berkeley, School of Law.

Michael plays guitar, holds a black belt in karate, is a workout junkie, and plays pickleball and hikes regularly in the hills and mountains of California and Colorado. He lives in Marin County, California.

www.ingramcontent.com/pod-product-compliance
Lightning Source LLC
Chambersburg PA
CBHW060505130626
46553CB00002B/411